Crafting Christmas Gifts

25 adorable projects featuring angels, snowmen, reindeer and other yuletide favourites

D&C
David and Charles
ALIS

A DAVID & CHARLES BOOK

Copyright © J.W. Cappelens Forlag 2003
Originally published in Norway as *Jul Med Tildas Venner*

First published in the UK in 2006 by
David & Charles
David & Charles is an
F+W Publications Inc. company
4700 East Galbraith Road
Cincinnati, OH 45236

A catalogue record for this book is
available from the British Library.

ISBN-13: 978-0-7153-2550-6 paperback
ISBN-10: 0-7153-2550-7 paperback

Printed in Singapore by KHL Printing
Co Pte ltd
for David & Charles
Brunel House   Newton Abbot   Devon

Visit our website at
www.davidandcharles.co.uk

David & Charles books are available from
all good bookshops; alternatively you can
contact our Orderline on 0870 9908222 or

Welcome to my Christmas ...

I live on a small island, where memories of summer are never far away even in the middle of winter. At least, that is how it feels, with the boats turned upside down in the gardens and the seagulls making a ruckus, in spite of the blanket of snow covering everything up. At night the pilot boat can be heard, on its way to guide foreign ships into familiar ports. But Christmas it is, after all. A light and pleasant Christmas, inspired by this little island, where people are few and far between in winter, and packed tight as herrings in a barrel during summer.

Although not many of us spend the winter out here on the island, Christmas is very lively. Numbers increase as some people come down to their summer houses for the festive holiday season, and others return home to celebrate Christmas with their families. There is no shortage of Christmas fairs on an island where artisans and artists almost make up the majority. Frozen cold, we stomp our boots on the threshold to get the snow off, and enter the warm house. We are ready to be inspired by handmade creations, to chat with friends and acquaintances, eat home-made waffles and drink mulled wine. Maybe we will find some Christmas gifts.

On Christmas Eve everybody, regardless of faith and denomination, congregates at the little, white church to imbibe the atmosphere. The church is filled to overflowing, with latecomers finding standing room only. The young and the old meet here, chatting about the events of the year gone by, providing insights into island life while the spirit and peace of Christmas slowly descends upon us.

Christmas on my small island, and a collection of lovely fabrics, are the inspiration for this book. First and foremost for those who like sewing, but there are craft projects in here for the rest of you, as well.

There are new variations of figures such as Santas, angels, reindeer and snowmen, and even penguins take centre stage in this book to wish you a creative pre-Christmas season, and a very merry Christmas!

Best regards

Contents

Many thanks to:

Nina, Robin, Eirin, Vanessa, Kari, Lollo, Torje and Matti for all the help they have given me in connection with this book.

I would also like to thank Ingrid Skaansar, Grethe Syvertsen Arnstad, Vibeke Sundbye, Merethe Lynghaug and Karin Mundal at Cappelen for their wonderful cooperation. Another thank you goes to all the contributors to this book.

The book was photographed in the old shop at Kilen gallery in Hvasser, using props and accessories from Tinnie's House in Tønsberg and the Lantern at Tjøme.

Fabrics and materials

Fabrics

Fabrics with a slightly coarse weave are better suited for sewing stuffed figures than very thin fabrics. They are easier to shape, as well as firmer, and thus help form a better shape.

Linen and plain cotton fabrics are mainly used for the stuffed figures. Fabrics with a woven pattern are often preferable to printed patterns. If you want to use thinner fabrics with printed patterns you may find it an advantage to iron a layer of fusible interfacing on the wrong side, to give you a firmer fabric.

Linen and plain cotton fabrics can be found in the fabric section of department stores and in hobby shops.

A variety of checks, stripes and fabrics in other patterns can also be found in shops that supply quilting and patchwork fabrics. You could also try shops that sell fabrics for curtains and upholstery. These are often a good source of stripes in different widths

as well as classic check patterns and French Toile for making stuffed figures.

The designs that do not require stuffing, as well as the clothes for the figures and the appliqués, can be made from all kinds of fabrics.

To make the fair skin for angels and Santas we have used a pale linen fabric. For darker skin we have used light brown linen.

Hair

Curly toy hair can be bought from craft and hobby shops. There are often good alternatives to be found in knitting yarn shops.

Wadding

There are many different kinds of wadding, but the one we have used is a synthetic middle-weight wadding which is thinner and firmer than light-weight wadding. You will find a good selection of waddings in most quilting and patchwork shops.

Fusible interfacing

Medium and lightweight interfacing is used. Both can have adhesive on one or both sides and are ironed on to fabric to give it body or to bond two fabrics.

Iron-on tape

This tape is useful for hemming clothes. Simply fold up the hem, insert lengths of tape and iron to bond.

Accessories

Natural materials, beads, thin steel wire, clothes hangers, glitter spray, boxes, paper and paints can be acquired through hobby shops.

A list of shops and mail order suppliers is given at the end of the book.

Making a good stuffed figure

Fabrics used for the stuffed figures in the book:

- Rocking reindeer: brown linen
- Santas and angels: skin-coloured and light brown linen
- Snowmen (all variations): natural white cotton
- Hearts: all kinds of fabrics, thin fabrics are reinforced using interfacing on the large and medium hearts
- Mice: skin-coloured, white and light brown linen, sand coloured cotton
- Gingerbread men: skin-coloured, light brown and brown linen
- Penguins: black and natural white, plain cotton
- Christmas trees: light green linen

Useful tools:

- Fine waterproof fabric pen, or a washable disappearing ink pen to trace the pattern on to the fabric. A white gel roller-ball pen or similar can be used for dark fabrics.
- Small, pointed fabric scissors
- A transparent sewing machine foot will make it easier to see and follow the pattern that has been traced on the fabric.
- Wooden plant stick (sanded down a little on the tip) is very useful for turning your figures the right way out and inserting stuffing.

Method:

1. Trace the pattern and sew

Do not cut the pieces from the fabric before sewing, instead fold the fabric in half and trace the patterns on to the fabric following the template. Mark any openings for turning the figures inside out or for padding, if these have been marked in the seam of the template. If the opening has been marked inside the pattern, there will be no seam openings.

Sew on the traced line. Use stitch lengths of 1.5–2mm ($^1/_{16}$in), and be careful to avoid any unevenness. See figure A.

2. Cutting out

Cut out the pieces, adding a small seam allowance, 3mm ($^1/_8$in) will do. However, a larger seam allowance of about 7–8mm ($^1/_4$in) must be cut where there are openings in the seam.

Where the opening is shown inside the pattern piece it is cut through one layer of fabric only.

Cut notches into the seam allowance where the seams curve inwards, see figure B.

3. Turning

A wooden plant stick is a good tool for turning your figures the right way out and for padding.

A

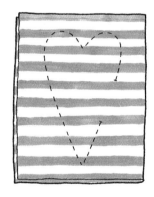 

B

Sand one end down a little, to avoid splinters snagging the fabrics.

As the seam allowances are so small, the figures must be turned right side out very carefully. Slide the plant stick along the inside of the seam after the figure has been turned out, to bring out all the details.

4. Iron

Fold the extra seam allowance at the openings into the figure and finger press. This does not apply to the extra seam allowance on the top of arms and legs, where they will go into the body. Always iron the figure before it is stuffed, see figure C.

5. Stuffing

Insert the stuffing loosely and gently into the figure, making sure it does not form lumps before it has been pushed into place. However, for small details, such as the noses for angels or Santas, shape a small piece of stuffing and push it into place before filling the rest of the figure.

Push the stuffing gently, but carefully, into place, adding more until your figure is nice and firm. The arms for the Santas, angels and pyjama snowmen are only stuffed in the lower parts so that they hang nicely, and can be bent easily, once the figure has been dressed.

Note that stuffing comes in many qualities. A good quality stuffing should not form lumps too easily,

nor be too smooth, but somewhere in between. Avoid upholstery wadding that may have lumps and do not use layered wadding to stuff figures.

6. Sewing up

Hand sew the openings closed, see figure D.

It may be worth spending time making a pretty seam in places where the opening will show, on the sides of the hearts, the belly of the reindeer, etc. If the sewn-up opening seems a bit hollow compared to the rest of the figure, try pulling the fabric and massaging the figure a little to improve the shape.

Detailed instructions for making the figures are given with each pattern.

C

D
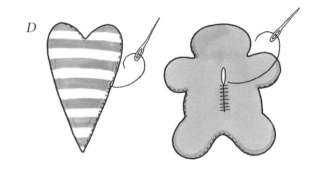

Faces

Put off adding face details until you have the ears, hair and hat in place. Then it is easier to see where the eyes should go.

You will need: a large-headed pin, black paint, a stamp pad in a muted pink colour (old-rose is best), and a brush. (You can use a lipstick instead of the stamp pad.)

Make rosy cheeks by gently brushing on the colour. Dip the pin head in black paint and stamp on eyes on either side of the face, dip once for each eye. Clean the pin afterwards.

Fabric noses

Iron double-sided interfacing on to the wrong side of the nose fabric. Cut out the nose following the pattern, remove the backing and iron it on to the figure before stuffing.

Carrot noses and penguin beaks

Plant sticks have been used to make the carrot noses and beaks for the stuffed figures. Use 3–4mm (⅛) diameter for small figures, 5–6mm (¼) diameter for larger figures such as the pyjama

snowmen, tea cosy snowman and the large penguins. Use a pencil sharpener to make a pointed end on the sticks and sand them down a little, for a smoother end result.

Paint the nose or beak (we have used a terracotta paint). Let the painted tip dry completely before cutting it to length with a knife.

Glue the nose/beak to the figure using a craft glue.

Sew fabric carrot noses and beaks on the appliquéd figures using a matching sewing thread.

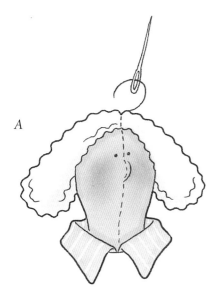

A

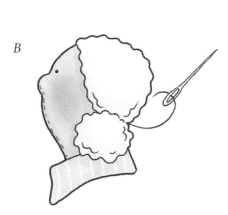

B

Hair

Toy hair comes in several colours; we have used white, blonde, auburn and brown for the Santas and angels.

Wind the hair around your hand to form a bunch that is 10–11cm (4–4½in) long for the angels and Santas in the small pattern size, 14–15cm (5½–6in) long for large Santas and angels and 8–9cm (3–3½in) long for the cornet angels.

Place the hair centrally on the head. If the figure has a hat, it is sufficient to tack down the hat to fasten the hair. On figures with no hat, stitch a central seam from the forehead down to the neck, see figure A. Smooth the hair down on either side and tack it around the back of the neck, see figure B.

Of course, you can easily make other hairstyles than the one shown here.

Frosting

Some of the figures have been given an attractive frost finish. To do this, you will need white fabric paint, or white water-based paint suitable for painting twigs, wood, etc. Also a flat brush and glitter spray suitable for fabrics. Buy a crystal coloured spray as coloured glitter sprays may just be too much.

Dip the dry brush in the fabric paint, and dab some of it off on a paper or such, until there is only a little paint left on the brush. Then brush the paint on to the figure with swift brush strokes, to and fro. Repeat if you want to make a stronger impact.

To make a frosted finish on garlands, wreaths, branches and such like that are not made from fabric, it is better to use a water-based hobby paint. The method is the same.

Finally, mask off any areas not to be sprayed and spray the model with glitter. There is no problem using fabric glitter spray on some other materials such as the craft ball snowmen, wreaths and so on.

Glitter spray used on its own will also make a nice finish on models where a painted frosting finish would not look right.

Decorative stitches

For clothes for the figures and other items such as the Christmas stockings, wall-hangings and hearts, simple running stitches have been sewn along the edges in a contrast colour. These stitches serve no other purpose than being decorative and it is important to keep them straight and even for the best effect.

On the clothes for the large Santas and the Christmas stockings, larger stitches, using embroidery yarn achieve a bold effect, while quilting thread or a double sewing thread has been used for the smaller models. In most cases, the seams have been a final finishing touch where needed, added after the model has been completed.

Decorative stitches on clothes must be added before the figure is dressed.

Quilting

The Christmas hangings have been quilted along the edges of the background, and these stitches go through all the layers. They help to keep the fabrics and wadding fixed together as is traditional for quilting.

Rocking reindeer

Pattern given on page 76.

You will need:

- brown linen or similar and interfacing for the body
- skin-coloured linen or similar for the antlers
- cotton fabric for the nose and ear linings
- lightweight interfacing
- stuffing
- wadding
- thin cord or string for the reins
- twigs, red beads and thin steel wire for the wreath
- small padded heart, see page 27
- simple wooden clothes hangers, plant stick 5–6mm (¼in) thick, small nails, paint and wood glue for the runners
- embroidery threads and fabric paints for the face

This is how you do it:

Reindeer

Read the general instructions for making stuffed figures on page 5. The rather complex shape of the reindeers means it is a good idea to reinforce the fabric with lightweight interfacing.

Iron the interfacing to the wrong side of the fabric for the body, and fold it right sides together. Trace the pattern for the body and legs.

Place a piece of brown linen body fabric (without interfacing) and a piece of ear lining fabric right sides together on top of a piece of wadding. Trace the ear pattern.

Fold a piece of pale linen fabric for the antlers in half, right sides together, and trace the antlers.

Sew around all the pieces, leaving openings as marked, see figure A.

Cut out the pieces, and cut an opening through one of the fabric layers of the legs, as shown on the pattern. Turn the pieces the right way out and iron. Add the nose. Fill the body, legs and antlers with stuffing and then sew the openings shut.

Tuck in the seam allowance along the bottom of the ears and fold them in half. Stitch the ears on to the head, see figure B. Sew the antlers to the back of the head, and the legs firmly on to the body. Sew a cross on the top of each leg, using an embroidery thread, to decorate, see figure C.

Paint the face as described on page 6.

Tie a length of cord/string around the muzzle, and attach a longer string on to each side for reins, see figure D. Twist a few twigs around the antlers and attach some beads, as described under Wreath on page 18. Add a small padded heart, see page 27.

Runners

Measure 4.5cm (2in) in from each end of the two clothes hangers, and mark the points.

Carefully hammer a small nail through each point, so that the tip of the nail sticks out on the other side of the hanger. Cut off two 6cm (2½in) lengths from the plant stick, and put some glue on either end.

Press the plant sticks on to the nail tips so that the stick and glue is pressed against the clothes hanger, see figure E.

Glue the legs on to the runners.

A

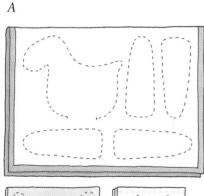

B

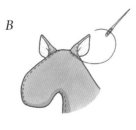

C

D

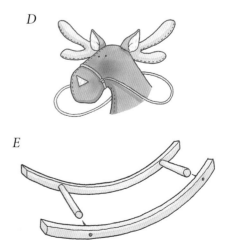

E

These deer have been given clothes hangers for runners, to make them into rocking reindeer. Of course, they can simply be made without the runners.

Santas

Pattern for the body given on page 77 and clothes on pages 77-79.

> **You will need:**
> - skin-coloured linen for bodies, arms and legs, or similar
> - various fabrics for the clothes
> - stuffing
> - interfacing
> - toy hair or similar
> - buttons
> - small hearts, see page 27
> - embroidery threads and fabric paints for the face

The small Santas are made from the pattern in this book. To make the bigger Santas you will need to enlarge the pattern on a photocopier or a scanner. Set the photocopier or scanner to 130% to achieve the size we have made here.

(Copy centres and libraries offer photocopying facilities and will often allow you to use their photocopier).

The clothes for the Santas can be varied according to your wish.

In our picture the big Santa boy is wearing a jacket without pockets, and a red linen hat with decorative stitching. The big Santa girl is wearing a coat with appliquéd hearts and decorative stitching. Both of them are wearing boots.

The little Santa girl is wearing a dress and apron with a pocket and the little Santa boy is wearing a coat in sand-coloured linen, with a pocket. Each of them has a small padded heart in their pockets.

All the hats are pulled well down on the heads and stitched to hold the hair in position as described on page 7.

On the following pages you will find the instructions on how to make the different clothes.

Make the faces as described on page 6 after fixing the hat.

Using just four colour-matched fabrics allows you to ring the changes for this family of Santas.

If you want the Santa to cover his mouth, make sure to twist his arm around inside the sleeve to get the thumb pointing upwards. Place the hand over the mouth, and stitch down, see the figure below.

Body

(The bodies of the large and small Santas, angels on page 17 and the good-night angels on page 19 are all made in the same way using the patterns on pages 77-79.)

Read the general instructions for making stuffed figures on page 5. The big Santas have stockings and boots, while the small Santas and all the angels have a simpler version, with the whole legs made from skin-coloured fabric.

To make the Santas with the boots and stockings, begin by sewing together a strip of shoe fabric and a strip of stocking fabric. Press the seam open and fold the joined-up strip over, right sides together. Trace the leg patterns so that the join between the fabrics matches the line on the pattern and sew around them, see figure A.

Fold the skin-coloured fabric over double and trace the body, arms and legs if the simple variation is needed. Sew around the edges, see figure B. Cut out the pieces, remembering to add an extra seam allowance for the openings. Turn right sides out, iron and stuff as described on page 5. Only the lower part of the arms should be padded to make the arms hang nicely.

Insert the seam allowance at the top of the legs into the opening at the bottom of the body, and sew the opening closed, fastening the legs as you go. Fold in the seam allowance at the top of the arms and stitch to the body, see figure C.

Clothes

Unlike the stuffed figures, it may be best to cut out the pieces for the clothes in advance. The exception is the collar. On page 7 you can read more about the decorative stitches that have been used on some of the clothes.

Dress

(The dress for the Santas, the angels on page 17 and the good-night angels on page 19 are all made in the same way.)

Cut out the two identical dress pieces and two sleeves, following the pattern. Add extra seam allowance at the bottom of the dress and ends of the sleeves. Sew the dress together across the shoulders, open out and sew in the sleeves, see figure A.

Fold the dress, right sides together, and sew up the sides and along the sleeves, see figure B.

Fold up the hem at the bottom of the dress and sleeves. Cut strips of iron-on tape and place them inside the hems. Iron to fasten, see figure C.

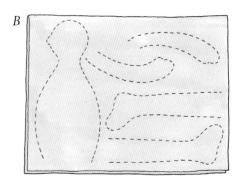

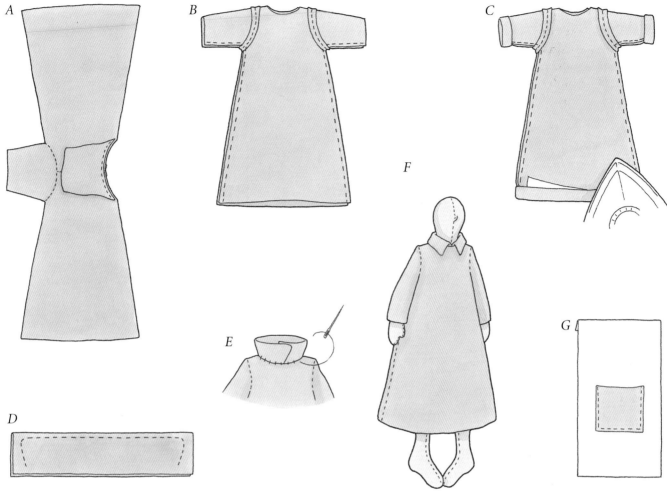

Fold the collar fabric in half and trace the collar. Sew around it, see figure D. Cut it out, turn right side out and iron the collar.

Turn the dress right sides out and tuck in the seam allowance around the neckline. Fit the collar into the neckline and stitch, see figure E. Fold the collar down, and iron the dress.

Put the dress on the stuffed figure, see figure F.

Apron

(The apron for the mother and daughter Santas and the angels on page 17 is made in the same way.)

Trace the apron and the pocket on to the fabric, and cut out, adding a good seam allowance. Turn up and hem the seam allowances using iron-on tape, as described for the hem on the dress.

Sew the pocket on to the apron, see figure G.

Make a small tuck on either side of the top of the apron and stitch it to the dress, see figure H.

Jacket/coat

(The jacket and coat for the Santas and the pyjama snowmen on page 23 are made in the same way.)

Fold the collar fabric in half and trace the pattern. Sew around it and cut out.

Cut out one pattern piece for the back, two for the front and two sleeves for the jacket or coat. Add extra seam allowances at the bottom of the front and back, and the ends of the sleeves.

(continued …)

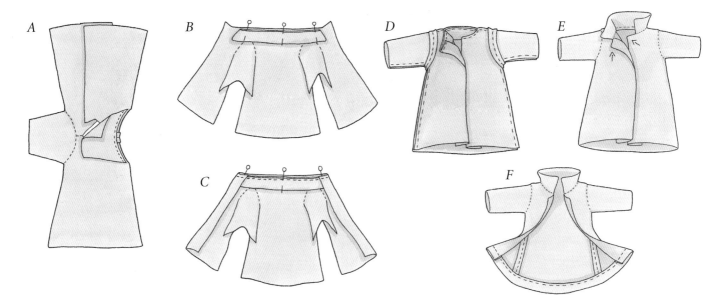

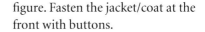

Sew the back and the two front pieces together across the shoulders, open out and sew in the sleeves, see figure A. Press seams open.

Pull the front pieces out to each side, so that the neck line is extended, and pin the collar to the right side of the coat, see figure B.

Fold the front facings right sides together along the dotted line and then sew across the facings and collar, see figure C.

Place the front pieces right sides together over the back piece, and sew together up the sides and along the sleeves of the jacket/coat, see figure D.

Turn up the hems of the sleeves and fix using iron-on tape. Turn the jacket/coat right side out. Carefully push out the tips of the facings that are formed on either side of the collar, see figure E.

Fold up the seam allowance at the bottom of the jacket/coat, and fold in the lower part of the front facings. Sew along the hem, see figure F.

Add a pocket, if you wish, or an appliquéd heart. The pocket is made the same way as the pocket on the apron.

For instructions on appliqué, see page 34.

Iron the jacket/coat, and dress the figure. Fasten the jacket/coat at the front with buttons.

Trousers

(The trousers for the Santas, the pyjama snowmen on page 23 and the mice on page 29 are all made in the same way.)

Cut out the pattern for the trousers adding an extra seam allowance at the waist and the hem of the trouser legs. Note that the straight edge of the pattern is placed on the fold of the fabric, see figure A. Make a note of the waist and hem on the trousers.

Place the two trouser pieces right sides together and stitch as shown in figure B. Press seams open. Fold the trousers the opposite way, matching the seams, and sew the legs as shown on figure C.

Turn up the hem at the bottom of the trousers and insert strips of iron-on tape. Iron to fix. Turn and press down the seam allowance around the waist (without tape), and put the trousers on the figure. Make tucks around the waist, if necessary, and sew the trousers on to the waist, see figure D.

(If you are making the trousers with braces for the mice, note that the braces must be placed inside on the back before the trousers are tacked on, see page 30.)

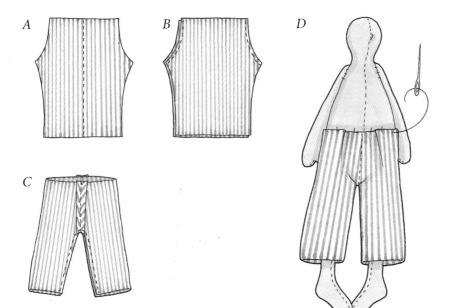

Hat

(The hats/nightcaps for the Santas, angels on page 19, pyjama snowmen on page 23 and the mice on page 29 are all made in the same way.)

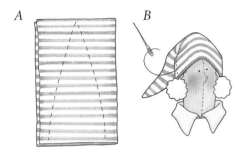

Fold the fabric for the hat/nightcap in half, trace the pattern and add extra seam allowance at the bottom. Sew around it, see figure A. Cut out and turn right side out. Fold in the seam allowance at the bottom, and iron before putting the hat on the figure. Tack the hat on to the head with a few stitches at the back and on either side.

To make the hats for the Santas and the mice fold down to one side, they need to be tacked down with a few stitches, see figure B. The nightcap is long enough to hang down on its own accord.

Scarf

(These instructions apply to the scarves for all the three-dimensional figures.)

All the scarves in this book are made from a length of fabric folded in half lengthways and pressed. Always cut along the grain of the fabric to prevent the edges from fraying or insert a strip of iron-on tape between the edges to join them. This is particularly important if you are using fabrics that fray easily or very fine fabrics.

Cut out the scarf for your figure using the measurements below.

Add a little seam allowance to the width of the scarf if you intend to use iron-on tape. After the edges have been

joined you can trim away the seam allowance, as the glue will prevent the edges from fraying.

Tie the scarf on to the figure. You can use a little fabric glue to fasten the long ends of the scarf to make it hang nicely. Cut the scarf to size if you think it is too long.

The scarves for the small snowmen, craft ball snowmen and the small

penguins have been cut to a size of about 4.5cm (2in) wide and 30–40cm (8–12in) long.

Scarves for the medium and large penguins and the big Santa are about 7.5cm (3in) wide and 45–55cm (18-22in) long.

The big scarf for the tea cosy snowman is about 10cm (4in) wide and 70cm (27½in) long.

Christmas angels in the kitchen. The festive biscuits are all baked, and put into the glass jars but one worried little angel is wondering whether she mistook salt for sugar in the macaroons.

Angels

Pattern for the body given on page 77 and for the clothes on pages 77–79.
A plywood heart wreath may be purchased from craft or hobby shops.

You will need:

- skin-coloured and light brown linen for bodies, arms and legs
- various fabrics for the clothes
- plain fabric for the wings
- iron-on tape
- stuffing
- wadding
- toy hair, blond and dark
- twigs, red beads and thin steel wire for wreath
- embroidery threads and fabric paints for the face

This is how you do it:

The little angel is made from the pattern in the book. To make the large angel the pattern must be enlarged, see page 10.

Make the body, dress and apron as described on pages 12 and 13.

Dress the angel before you attach the hair, see page 7, and make the face as described on page 6.

If you want to fasten the angel's hand over its mouth, follow the instructions for the Santas, on page 12.

Wings

The wings for the angels, good-night angels on page 19, angel pyjama snowmen on page 23, angel mice on page 28, cornet angel on page 32, angel snowmen on page 64 and angel penguins on page 68 are all made in the same way. The big angel uses three layers of wadding and the small wings of the snow angels on page 62 and the angel penguins on page 68 only need one layer. The rest have two layers.

Fold the wing fabric in half, right sides together, and place the wadding underneath. Trace the wing pattern

and sew around, see figure A. Cut out the wings, and cut notches in the seam allowance where the seams swing inwards. Cut an opening through one layer of the fabric, as shown on the pattern. Turn right sides out, and iron the wings. If you wish, you can add decorative stitches or quilt around the edge of the wings. Stitch the wings on to the figure with the opening facing the back, so that it is hidden.

A

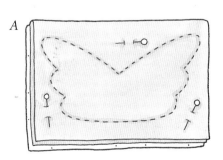

A little angel sits here, looking as if she is miles away. Maybe she's dreaming about a new dress for Christmas? It would be nice if she was around all through the year, and not just at Christmas.

Wreaths

The wreaths on the models in this book have been made from tiny twigs.

Make a little wreath from the twigs twisting thin steel wire around to hold them all together. Thread red beads one by one on another length of steel wire, twisting the wire around the beads as they are threaded, so that they stay in place, see figure B. Wind the steel wire with the beads around the twig wreath. The beads could also be glued directly on to the twigs, but will not stay on quite as well.

Glue or stitch the wreath on to the head, see figure C.

B

C

Good-night angels

Pattern for the body given on page 77 and for the clothes on pages 77–79.

You will need:

- skin-coloured and light brown linen for bodies, arms and legs
- various fabrics for the clothes
- iron-on tape
- plain fabric for the wings
- stuffing
- wadding
- toy hair, white and dark brown
- buttons
- embroidery threads and fabric paints for the face

This is how you do it:

Make the body and the dress (without the apron) as described on page 12. Make the wings as described on page 17, and the nightcap as described on page 15.

Put the dress on the figure, and fasten it with stitched on buttons. Attach the wings. Make the hair as described on page 7 and tack on the hat with a few stitches on either side, see page 15.

Add a face for the angel as described on page 6.

Pillow

Fold the fabric for the pillow in half, right sides together. Trace the pattern and sew around it. Cut it out and cut an opening through one layer of fabric where marked on the pattern. Turn the right way out, iron and fill the pillow with stuffing. Stitch the pillow on to the figure and the hand to the pillow, so that the angel appears to be holding it. Fasten the other hand to the face as described for Santas on page 12, see the figure below.

It is not easy to go to sleep the night before Christmas when there is so much to look forward to. The good-night angels might help you drop off and could hang out throughout the year. They would, of course, also make lovely gifts.

*The days after Christmas
often start with a late
breakfast in bed and it is
perfectly acceptable to watch a
nice film on TV still dressed in
pyjamas, with a box of sweets
in your lap, before getting all
dressed up again. Therefore, it
is quite appropriate that some
of the figures in this book are
still in their pyjamas, joining
in with the relaxed Christmas
spirit. These pyjama snowmen
match the good-night angels,
perhaps as a gift for a little
boy.*

Pyjama snowmen

Pattern given on page 80.

You will need:

- natural white cotton for the bodies, arms and legs
- various fabrics for the pyjamas
- iron-on tape
- stuffing
- buttons for the jacket and ear-muffs
- plant stick for the carrot nose, see page 6
- thin cord or string
- fabric and wadding for the wings (optional)
- twigs, beads and thin steel wire for the wreath
- embroidery threads and fabric paints for the face

This is how you do it:

Read the general instructions for stuffed figures on page 5.

Fold the white cotton in half and trace the patterns for the body, arms and legs. Mark the seam openings as shown on the pattern and sew around. Cut out the pieces, adding seam allowances. Turn the arms and legs right side out and iron. Only the lower parts of the arms should be stuffed, and the legs should be loosely stuffed in the top parts. Insert the arms into the body through the shoulder openings and sew them on, see figure A.

Take hold of the arms and pull them out through one of the leg openings, so that the figure is turned right side out. Iron the body and fill it with stuffing. Insert the legs into the corresponding openings on the body and sew them on, see figure B.

Make the pyjama jacket following the instructions for the jacket/coat on page 13 and the trousers as described on page 14. Add an appliqué heart or decorative stitching if you wish.

Dress the figure and make the face as described on page 6. Glue on the nose. Sew on buttons for the ear-muffs.

Raise one arm up behind the head, and stitch it on to the back of the head. Sew a cord/string loop to the back of the hand to hang it from. Put the other hand up against the mouth to stifle a yawn and stitch it on just underneath the nose, see figure C.

The angel version is made by giving the pyjama snowman wings and a wreath. The wings are the same as used for the angels, see the instructions for wings on page 17 and the wreath on page 18.

A

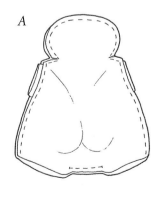

B

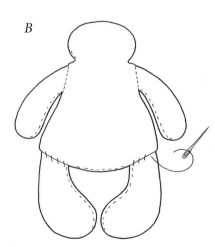

C

Hearts

Pattern is given on page 81.

There is no Christmas without putting a heart into it.

Large hearts with wings make simple and attractive decorations, which can be hung casually on pegs and door handles. The medium-sized hearts look good on the Christmas tree and on wreaths. The small hearts have a whole range of uses, including napkin rings and gift ties and are seen on many of the figures in this book.

Winged hearts

This is how you do it:

Read the general instructions for making stuffed figures on page 5.

If you want to make the heart from thin fabric, reinforce it by ironing interfacing to the wrong side first.

Fold the fabric right sides together, and trace the heart pattern. Mark the openings for the wings and for turning the heart the right way out, and then sew around the edge, see figure A.

Fold the fabric for the wings right sides together, and place two layers of wadding underneath. Trace two wings following the pattern, and sew around them, see figure B.

Cut out the heart and the wings. Turn the wings the right way out and iron them. Put them inside the heart, and sew them on, see figure C. Cut away the extra seam allowance along the edge where the wings are attached. Turn the heart right sides out and fill it firmly with stuffing, following the instructions on page 6. Stitch the opening closed. Attach a ribbon or cord from the top to hang it from, see figure D.

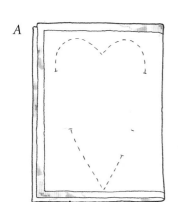

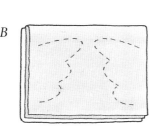

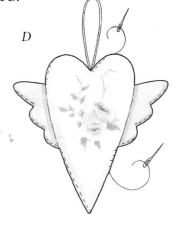

Small and medium hearts

If the fabric is thin, reinforce it with iron-on interfacing before sewing and cutting out as it gives a better shape, although it is not always absolutely necessary.

If the hearts are going to decorate a wreath or a figure where the back of the heart is hidden from view, the opening for turning the sewn piece the right way out can be cut through one layer of fabric in the middle of the heart. If the back of the heart is going to show, the opening should be in the seam on the side of the heart.

Fold the fabric in half, right sides together, and trace the pattern. Sew round the edge, cut it out, turn the right way out and iron. Fill with stuffing and stitch the opening shut, as in the instructions on pages 5 and 6.

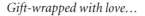

Gift-wrapped with love…

The angel mice are made from the large pattern which means the angel wings will fit. See page 18 for how to make the wreath.

Mice

Pattern given on pages 82–83.

You will need:

- skin-coloured, sand-coloured or brown linen for the heads, hands, legs, ears and wings
- cotton lining fabric for the ears
- red cotton fabric for the nose
- iron-on tape
- various fabrics for the clothes
- stuffing
- wadding
- buttons
- embroidery threads and fabric paints for the face

This is how you do it:

Please note that the mice and their clothes come in two sizes.

Body

Read the general instructions for making stuffed figures on page 5.

Sew together a strip of heads and hands fabric with a strip of sweater fabric, press the seam open and then fold the whole strip in half, right sides together. Trace the body and arm patterns so that the join between the fabrics matches the line on the pattern.

Sew around the pieces, see figure A.

Place a piece of ear fabric and a piece of ear lining fabric right sides together, with a layer of wadding underneath. Trace the ear pattern and sew around, see figure B.

Fold the fabric for the legs in half, trace the pattern and sew around.

Cut out, turn right sides out and iron all pieces. Fill the body, arms and legs with stuffing, see page 6.

Insert the legs in the openings for them on the body, and sew the opening closed so that the legs are fastened.

Tack on the arms. See figure C.

Fold in the seam allowance around the opening for the ears, and fold them in half.

If you would like your mouse to have a hat, follow the instructions on page 15, and attach it to the head. Stitch the ears to the head on the outside of the hat, see picture above. If the mouse does not have a hat, the ears are attached to the head as shown in figure D.

Make the face as described on page 6 and stick on a nose.

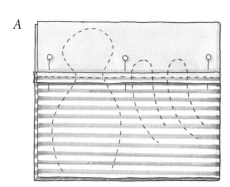

A

B

C

D

Clothes

Note that one edge of the braces pattern should be placed on the folded edge of the fabric. Opened out the folded edge is in the middle, see figure E. Fold the braces in half, right sides together, and sew as shown in figure F. Turn the right way out and iron.

Cut out the skirt pieces following the pattern, adding an extra seam allowance at the top and bottom for turning in.

Make a pocket as for the apron on page 13, and sew it on to one part of the skirt. Place the skirt pieces right sides together, and sew the side seams, see figure G. Press the seams open and then turn up the hem and fix with iron-on tape as for the dress on page 12. Turn down the seam allowance at the top of the skirt (without any tape) and then turn the skirt right side out.

Trousers are made the same way as the trousers on page 14.

Dress the mouse in trousers or skirt, making a pleat each side, at the front as well as the back, to fit. Attach the open ends of the braces to the inside of the trousers/skirt at the back of the figure, crossing them over on the back, see figure H.

Use buttons to fasten the braces to the outside of the trousers/skirt on the front.

E

F

G

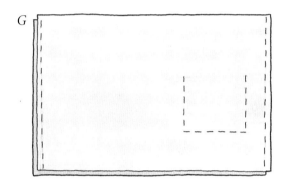

Christmas mouse infatuation …

30

H

A party of mice filling a wicker chair, and full of anticipation.
In this house there are no mousetraps, but plenty of biscuits.

Cornet angels

Pattern given on page 84.

You will need:

- skin-coloured, light and dark brown linen for faces
- various fabrics for the wings
- various fabrics and linings for the cornets
- wadding
- stuffing
- toy hair, blond, light and dark brown
- twigs, beads and thin steel wire for the wreath
- cord for hanging
- embroidery threads and fabric paints for the face

This is how you do it:

Note that the cornet pattern must be placed on the folded edge of the fabric which is double with right sides together. When opened out the fold is in the middle, see figure A.

Cut out one cornet in fabric, one in lining and two in wadding. The fabric and lining are placed on top of each other, right sides together. One piece of the wadding is placed underneath, the other on the top. Sew the parts together along the curved edge on the top of the cornet, see figure B. Unfold the cornet, so that the seam is across the middle, and fold it right sides together the opposite way. Sew as shown on figure C, leaving an opening in the lining. Trim any excessive seam allowances and turn the cornet right sides out. Sew the opening closed, and push the lining well into the fabric part, using a plant stick. Iron the cornet.

Fold the fabric for the head in half, right sides together, and trace the head pattern. Sew around it, cut out, turn the right way out, iron, fill with stuffing and stitch the opening, following the instructions on page 5, see figure D. Make the face, see page 6 and attach the hair, see page 7.

Make the wings as described on page 17. Tack them on to the cornet, so that the middle of the wings protrudes approximately 1cm (½in) above the edge of the cornet, see figure E. Stitch the head firmly on to both the cornet and the wings.

Use pins to fasten the cord on either side of the cornet. Adjust so that it hangs fairly straight. If the angel tips too far forwards or backwards, the cord must be adjusted accordingly, before it is stitched on.

A

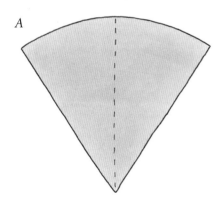

B

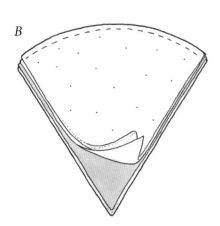

C

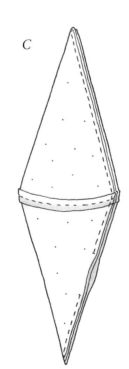

D

E

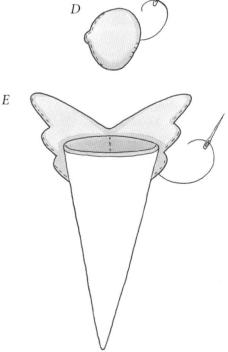

*A cornet angel will probably ponder
more than once, on the meaning of life.
Filled to the brim with all things sweet,
for others she is providing a treat.
She's wondering how well this will go,
a life of temptation, but hands? Oh no.*

Striking appliqués

Patterns given on pages 79 and 81 87.

You will need:

- various fabrics
- interfacing
- white fabric paint
- a flat brush (size 6–8)
- buttons and beads
- embroidery threads and fabric paints for the face

This is how you do it:

The appliqués have been lightly brushed with textile paint, giving a fine effect of frosting. This is not at all difficult, and gives the whole design more unity.

The designs consist of individual figures which can be put together in many different ways. Some combinations are shown in the illustrations, but feel free to use your imagination to make new designs.

The motifs for the appliqués are reversed in the pattern, because they are traced on to the wrong side of the fabrics. When turned over, they will correspond to the motifs in the pictures.

Iron double-sided interfacing on to the wrong side of the fabrics and pull off the paper.

Trace the pattern pieces for the motif on the interfaced side of the fabrics. Cut them out. Place the pieces on a sheet of paper, plastic tablecloth or similar, with the right side facing up.

Look at the picture of the motif of your choice, and see where the frosting has been added to the figures. Dip a dry brush into the fabric paint, and dab some of it off on a piece of paper, so that only a little of the paint is left on the brush. Brush the paint on to the fabric figures with light, swift strokes. Repeat the process if the paint effect seems too faint.

The raw edges may fray a little during this process. Wait until the paint has dried, and then trim the edges with a sharp pair of scissors.

Position the pieces of the motif on the intended background and iron them on. Sew around the figures using buttonhole stitches, either by hand or using the sewing machine.

The wording and decorative stitches on the appliqués can be made using either sewing thread or quilting thread.

Make the faces for the figures as described on page 6.

Do not stitch the beads or buttons on to the motif until you have completed the whole design, as they will be in the way when you iron it.

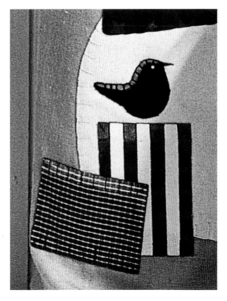

Christmas hanging with reindeer and sleigh

Patterns given on page 84 and 86.

You will need:

- fabric for the background, border and binding
- lightweight interfacing if one of the background fabrics is linen
- fabric for the backing
- wadding
- various fabrics for the appliqués, see page 34
- 3 or 4mm (¼in) red beads, 4mm (¼in) white beads and small light blue or lilac beads
- cord or string for the reins
- thin cord for the runners of the sleigh
- 24 large buttons
- embroidery threads

This is how you do it:

The hanging in the photo has a background of white and sand-coloured linen. Linen can lose its shape over a large area, which is why it is a good idea to iron some lightweight interfacing on to the back to make it firmer.

Add seam allowances to all the pieces described below.

The white background piece is 94 x 24cm (37 x 9½in). Cut two border strips of 94 x 8cm (37 x 3¼in) and sew on to the background, see figure A. Then cut two border strips of 40 x 8cm (16 x 3¼in) and sew them on to the sides, see figure B.

The motif consists of three reindeer with collars and a sleigh with presents.

Appliqué the motif on to the background, as described on page 34.

Using three strands of embroidery yarn sew a large cross at the top of the reindeer legs, sew the twig decorations on to the antlers, and embroider 'Merry Christmas' in black thread. The ribbons on the presents and decorative stitches around the sign and parcel can be sewn on using either quilting thread or sewing cotton. Do not sew on the beads, runners and reins yet.

The fabric for the backing and the wadding is cut out measuring 110 x 40cm (43½ x 16in).

Pin together the appliqué, wadding and backing. Quilt around the white background using even running stitches as shown on the hanging in the picture, to hold the layers in place. Use a sewing machine if you do not want to quilt by hand.

Make a binding for the hanging as described on page 38, sew on the beads, reins, and runners. Attach 24 buttons around the outer border using red embroidery yarn tied in a knot.

For the small sacks, see page 52.

Display

The Christmas hanging can be hung on the wall using plastic or brass rings sewn on along the top. If you think the sacks are likely to be heavy when you have filled them, you can sew a casing along the top and insert a strip of wood or dowel rod on the back to support its weight, see page 38.

A

B

36

This Christmas hanging looks quite feminine due to the fabrics we have chosen. Other fabrics will give it a quite different character.

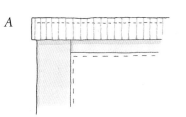

A

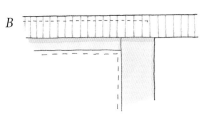

B

Binding

The hanging can be edged using bias binding, but there is more choice if it is edged with an attractive fabric as is the one in the picture.

Cut strips 4cm (1½in) wide, and join them up to form a strip long enough to frame the whole calendar. Start in one corner, placing the strip of fabric right side facing the right side of the hanging. Sew the strip on, about 6mm (¼in) from the edge, see figure A. When you reach a corner, stop the seam about 6mm (¼in) from the end, see figure B. Fold the strip as shown in figure C, before continuing the seam. Once the strip has been sewn all around the edge of the hanging, fold it over and stitch it down on the back, see figure D.

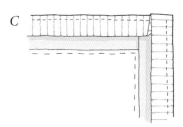

C

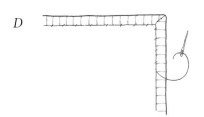

D

Casing for the strip of wood

Cut a strip of fabric that is 5cm (2in) wide plus seam allowances (to fit a strip of wood or a dowel of about 2cm/1in) by the finished width of the hanging.

Fold in the seam allowance, and tack on the strip about 1cm (½in) from the top edge, see figure A.

It is important to check that there is room for the wood strip before it is sewn down at the bottom. Also, push the fabric strip upwards, to make sure that it does not show over the top of the hanging. See figure B.

Attach an eye screw at either end of the hanging, going through the fabric casing and into the strip of wood.

A

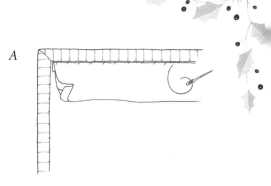

B

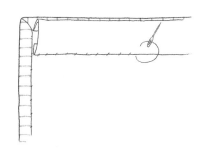

Christmas stockings

Patterns given on pages 85, 87 and 90.

We have made short and long Christmas stockings in two different versions. One has been given penguins as a motif, set on a greyish-blue background. The other has a motif of snowmen, with red as the main colour. Matching padded figures can be made to decorate a child's room, see page 62 and 67.

Short Christmas stockings

You will need:
- fabric for the stocking
- fabric for the lining
- wadding
- fabric and buttons for hanging loop
- various fabrics for appliqués, see page 34
- buttons, 3–4mm (¼in) red beads and small white seed beads for snowflakes
- embroidery yarns

These Christmas stockings have snowmen for their motifs and red as the main colour.

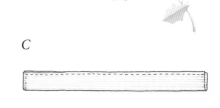

Short Christmas stockings

This is how you do it:

Add seam allowances to the pieces as described below.

Trace the bottom part of the stocking following the pattern, matching AA to BB and adding about 27cm (11in) to the length, see figure A. Cut out the stocking twice in fabric, lining and wadding. Appliqué the motif on to the stocking as the instructions on page 34. Note that each snowman and penguin have been marked to show where to end them if they are to be used as a motif coming out of a box. Do not attach the beads and buttons yet.

Place a piece of wadding on the wrong side of the stocking fabric and place the lining right sides together, against the fabric. Sew together along the top. Pull the fabric with wadding away from the lining. Do the same with the other three stocking pieces.

Place the two stocking pieces right sides together, and sew around them, see figure B. Leave an opening in the lining.

Turn the stocking right sides out, close the opening, and push the lining into the fabric part.

Iron the stocking, and fold the top part 7–8cm (3in) down over the outside, to show the lining. Sew on the beads and buttons. Add decorative stitches around the stocking using embroidery yarn, starting and finishing underneath the fold.

Cut a strip of fabric of about 35 x 7cm (14 x 3in). Fold in half lengthways, right sides together, and sew around, see figure C. Turn out and iron. Tuck in the seam allowance at the end before sewing up the opening.

Attach each end of the loop to the stocking with buttons, see figure D.

C

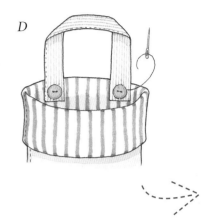

D

B

A

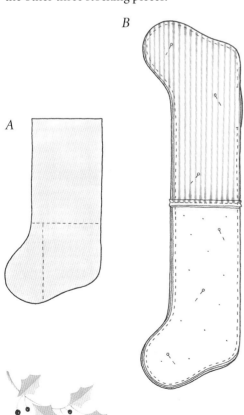

Long Christmas stockings

This is how you do it:

Add seam allowances to all the pieces described below.

Trace the foot, following the pattern and matching AA to BB and cut out two pieces from the fabric. Appliqué the patches for the heels using double-sided interfacing, see appliqués on page 34. Cut out two pieces measuring 21.5 x 60cm (8½ x 24in), for the upper part of the stocking and sew on to the foot pieces, see figure A.

Cut out two pieces corresponding to the entire stocking in the lining fabric, and cut out two pieces of the wadding, 1cm (½in) longer than the whole stocking.

Cut out the fabric for the pocket, adding an ample seam allowance. Cut out one pocket piece in wadding, without any seam allowance. Place the wadding on the wrong side of the fabric. Fold the seam allowance over the wadding, and tack it in place, see figure B.

Cut out the appliqué pieces, choosing the pattern line for the pocket, and appliqué the motif on to the pocket as described on page 34.

Sew the pocket centrally on one of the stocking parts.

E

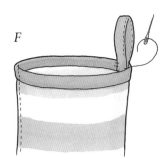

F

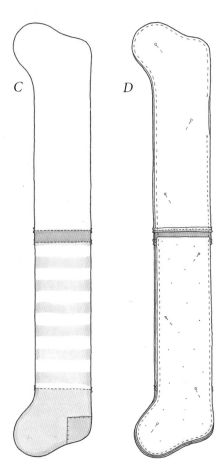
You will need:

- fabric for the foot and pocket
- fabric for the upper part of the stocking
- fabric for the lining
- fabric for binding and loop
- wadding
- various fabrics for appliqués, see page 34
- double-sided interfacing
- buttons, small white seed beads and 3–4mm (¼in) red beads
- embroidery yarns

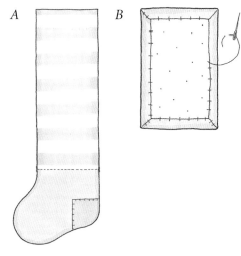

A   *B*

Cut two strips of 21.5 x 2cm (8½ x 1in), to form a binding at the top of the stocking and sew on to each of the stocking pieces. Sew the stocking linings on to the other side of the binding, see figure C.

Place the two fabric stocking parts with lining, right sides together and place the wadding on the wrong side of the fabric. Sew around, leaving an opening in the lining, see figure D. Turn the stocking right sides out, and sew decorative stitches on the foot, before the seam allowance is closed, so that the fastening knots can be hidden inside the stocking.

Push the lining into the fabric part, and iron the stocking. Sew the beads and buttons on to the pocket motif.

Loop

Cut a strip of fabric measuring 4 x 16cm (1¾ x 6½in) plus seam allowances to make a loop. Fold the strip in half, right sides together, and sew around it, see figure E. Turn the strip inside out, using a plant stick or similar. Iron the loop, and sew the opening closed, before sticking it on to the back of the stocking, see figure F.

These Christmas stockings have penguin motifs and a grey-blue main colourway. Matching stuffed penguins sit on the table nearby.

LEO

Christmas hanging with snowman and penguins

Patterns given on page 85, 86 and 87.

This is how you do it:

If required or made from linen, iron interfacing on to the wrong side of the background fabric.

Add seam allowances to all the pieces described below.

The centre background piece should measure 84 x 34cm (33 x 13½in). Cut two border strips of 84 x 8cm (33 x 3¼in) and sew on to the background, see figure A. Then cut out two border strips each measuring 50 x 8cm (20 x 3¼in) and sew them on to each side, see figure B.

See the illustration opposite for the figures required for the motif, and appliqué them on to the background fabric as described on page 34. Do not sew on the buttons and beads yet.

Cut out a piece of fabric for the backing, and a piece of wadding, to the size of 100 x 50cm (39½ x 20in).

Pin the front, wadding and backing fabric together. Quilt the border around the background as shown opposite, to hold the layers together. Use a sewing machine if you do not wish to hand-quilt your piece.

Make a binding for the hanging as described on page 38, and sew the beads and buttons on to the appliqué.

Attach 24 buttons around the border, using red embroidery yarn tied in a knot.

For the little sacks, see page 52.

The hanging can be hung on the wall using plastic or brass rings sewn on along the top. If you think the sacks are likely to be heavy you can make a casing along the top and insert a strip of wood or a dowel rod on the back, see page 38.

A

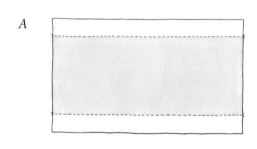

B

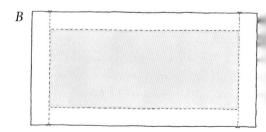

Two penguins, a snowman, some Christmas trees, gingerbread men, presents and birds are used to make up an entertaining Christmas motif.

Stylish wall bags

Patterns given on page 86 and 87.

Patterns given on page 86 and 87.

You will need:

- fabrics for the bag, pocket and lining
- fabric and 2 buttons for the hanging loops
- wadding
- various fabrics for the appliqués, see page 34
- a clothes hanger
- embroidery threads

This is how you do it:

Add seam allowances to all the pieces described below.

Cut out two pieces in the bag fabric, two in the lining and two pieces in wadding. They should be 46 x 34cm (18 x 13½in).

Place one piece of wadding on the wrong side of the fabric and the fabric and lining right sides together. Sew across the top. Do the same with the other three pieces.

Cut a pocket measuring 20 x 24cm (8 x 9½in) in fabric (with seam allowances) and wadding (without seam allowances) and make up as for the pocket on the long Christmas stocking on page 42. Appliqué the motifs on the pocket, following the instructions on page 34, and sew the pocket on to one of the outer fabric pieces. The distance from the sides and the bottom of the pocket should be roughly the same, see figure A.

Cut out a strip measuring 5 x 8cm (2 x 3¼in) and make a loop 2.5cm (1in) wide, following the instructions for the loop for the long Christmas stocking.

Place the fabric pieces with the lining right sides together, fold the strip for the loop over double and place it between the layers at the bottom of the bag. Sew around the edges, leaving an opening in the lining for turning the bag inside out, see figure B.

Turn the bag inside out, sew the opening closed, and push the lining into the fabric piece. Turn about 9cm (3½in) down to form a border showing the lining at the top of the bag and iron the bag. Appliqué a small name tag from the box on the folded-down border. The fastenings for the thread can be hidden underneath.

A

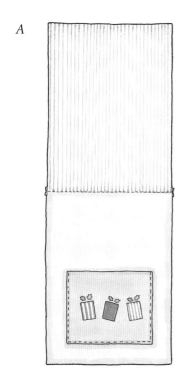

B

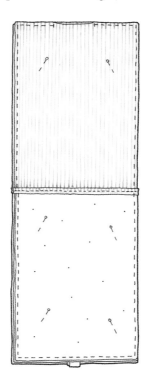

Cut two strips of fabric measuring 10 x 16cm (4 x 6½in) and make two 5cm (2in) wide loops in the same way as for the small loop. Fold in half and sew them firmly on to each side of the bag, about 5cm (2in) in from the sides and about 3–4cm (1½in) down. Add a button for decoration on each of the loops if you wish, see figure C. Hang the bag on the clothes hanger.

C

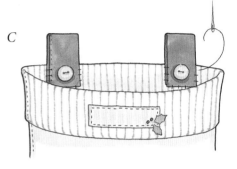

These clever little wall bags can be used for a number of purposes. If you make more than one, they can be hung underneath each other as we have done in the picture. The wall bag with gingerbread men on the pocket would do well for storing Christmas cookie recipes in the kitchen. Feel free to use other motifs than the ones we have used here.

This wall bag with a rocking reindeer motif is holding all the Christmas mail.

Gift sacks

This is how you do it:

Add seam allowances to all the parts that are described below.

Wine sack: cut two pieces of 18 x 40cm (7 x 16in) for the bag and a border strip of 36 x 16cm (14 x 6½in).

Gift sack: Cut out two pieces of 30 x 28cm (12 x 11in) and a border strip 56 x 16cm (22 x 5½in).

Appliqué a motif, if you wish, on one of the sack pieces, following the instructions on page 34. Position the motif about 7cm (3in) from the bottom of the sack.

Place the pieces for the sack right sides together and sew around three edges, see figure A.

Fold the fabric for the border in half, so that it is the same width as the sack. Sew it together as shown in figure B, with the seam starting about 2cm (1in) down from the top to make an opening in the casing. Press the seam allowance open, see figure C. Turn the top part of the border down, making it double, with the right side and the opening out. Make a seam for the casing around the border piece, about 2cm (1in) up from the bottom, see figure D.

Place the border inside the sack and sew the sack and border together. Add a zig-zag seam outside the seam if you like, to make sure the ends do not fray, see figure E.

Match the side and bottom seams together. Sew across each bottom corner, about 4cm (1½in) in from the tip, and cut away the corner outside the seam, see figure F.

Turn the bag right sides out, and thread a drawstring via the opening, through the casing so that the sack can be closed. If you like, attach a little padded heart to each end of the cord, see figure G and page 5.

You will need:

- fabric to make the sack
- fabric for the border
- ribbons or a cord
- various fabrics for appliqués, see page 34
- small padded hearts, see page 27
- embroidery threads

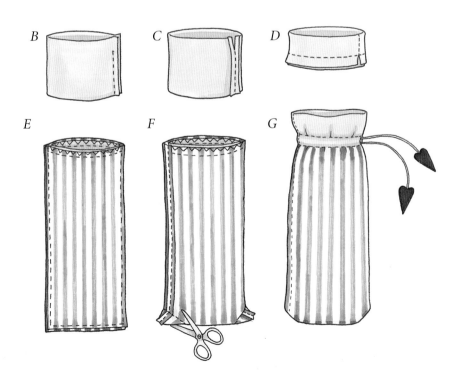

A   *B*   *C*   *D*

E   *F*   *G*

The gift sacks are presents in their own right, especially if they are decorated with appliqués. The sack without any motif is fairly quickly made, and a much simpler solution.

Small sacks

Patterns given on page 86.

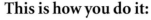

You will need:

- fabric for the sack
- raffia or ribbons
- various fabrics for appliqués, see page 34

This is how you do it:

Cut two pieces of fabric for the sack, both measuring 10 x 16cm (4 x 6½in), adding seam allowances with extra at the top. If you wish, you can appliqué a small motif on one piece, following the instructions on page 34. Place the pieces, right sides together, and sew around the sack, see figure A.

Fold the seam allowance at the top down twice so that the raw edges are hidden and sew around the hem, see figure B. Turn right sides out, and iron. Fill the sack and tie around the top with a length of raffia or a ribbon.

A

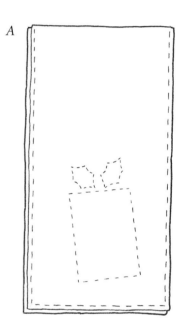

B

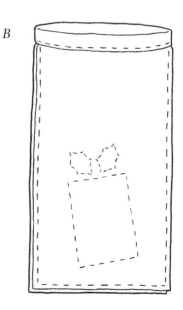

Little sacks, with or without motifs, can be used as lavender bags, filled with sweets or used as bags for the wall hangings, and come in very handy. At the very least they are fun to make, as they are so simple, and turn into such nice presents.

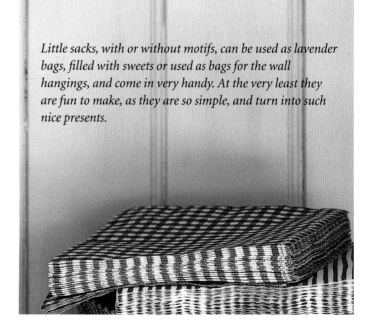

Snowman tea cosy

Pattern given on page 88.

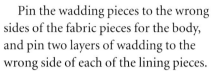

This is how you do it:

Body

Trace the pattern, matching AA with BB. The straight edge of the pattern must be placed on the folded edge of the fabric, see figure A.

The piece for the lining is traced the same way, but finished at the top following the curved dotted line, see figure B.

Cut out two pieces of fabric and two pieces of wadding to make the body, cut two pieces of the lining fabric and four pieces of wadding to make the lining.

Pin the wadding pieces to the wrong sides of the fabric pieces for the body, and pin two layers of wadding to the wrong side of each of the lining pieces.

Place the lining pieces right sides together on the body pieces, and sew along the curve at the bottom, see figure C.

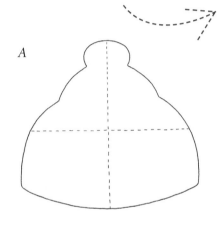

A

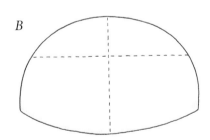

B

C

This snowman is not just decorative,
he is useful as well, hiding a teapot and
keeping the tea hot. He is helpful, too,
always ready with a napkin in case
somebody should be unfortunate enough
to spill some tea, and more than happy
to offer everybody a gingerbread cookie.

Fold the lining and body away from each other, and place the two body pieces with the lining right sides together. Sew around, leaving an opening in the lining, see figure D.

Trim the seam allowances, and cut notches where the seam makes an inward turn. Turn the right way out, and iron the snowman. Stuff the head and top part of the body and sew the opening closed. Push the lining into the body, see figure E.

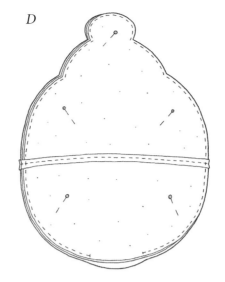

D

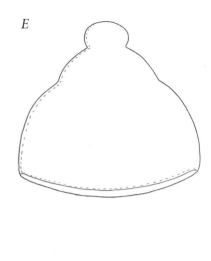

E

Jacket

The jacket is made without arms which are made separately and stitched on to the figure right at the end.

Cut out one piece of fabric for the back and two for the front of the jacket, and the same for the lining.

Place the front jacket pieces right sides together with the back piece and sew up the sides, see figure F. Do the same with the lining.

To make the collar, place one piece each of the jacket and lining material right sides together. Trace around the collar, and sew. Cut out, turn right sides out, and iron the collar.

Stretch out the neckline of the jacket and lining and place the jacket fabric and the lining right sides together. The collar is positioned between the two layers so that the outside fabrics go together, and the lining fabrics go together. Sew around as shown on figure G, leaving an opening for turning.

Turn the coat right side out, and iron. Sew up the opening.

Cut a strip of the loop fabric 2.5 x

F

G

14cm (1 x 5½in) plus seam allowances and make a loop as described for the long Christmas stocking on page 42. Stitch the loop on to the neck behind the top of the snowman's head.

Make a scarf as described on page 15. Tie the scarf on to the figure before putting on the jacket. Fasten in place by sewing two buttons on the front.

Sew on buttons for ear-muffs, and make the face with a carrot nose as described on page 6, see figure H.

H

Arms

Fold the fabric for the sleeves in half, and the same with the fabric for the hands. Trace the patterns and sew around, see figure I.

Cut out and turn the pieces the right way out. Fold in the seam allowance at the opening of the sleeves, and iron the sleeves and hands. Stuff the sleeves loosely and the hands. Insert the hands in the opening of the sleeves, and fasten with stitches, see figure J.

Make a gingerbread man as described on page 58, and a small heart as described on page 27. Cut out a piece of fabric, 11cm (4½in) square to for the napkin.

Stitch the sleeves on to the snowman at shoulder height. Place the ginger-bread man and napkin on the figure and stitch them on firmly before fastening the hands, so that they appear to be holding both the napkin and the gingerbread man.

Finally, stitch the little heart firmly to the jacket, see figure K.

When the tea cosy snowman needs a rest, he is happy to hang on a hook, as he does not want to get in anybody's way.

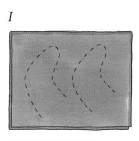

I

J

K

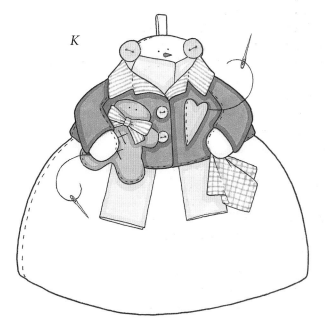

Gingerbread men

Pattern given on page 92.

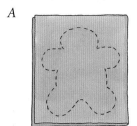

A gingerbread man is set in a wooden frame. The cardboard backing has been lined with fabric, and the gingerbread man glued down, wreathed with twigs. Holes drilled through the frame provide a way to hang the picture.

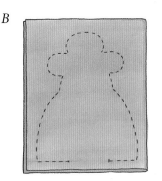

This is how you do it:

Body

Read the general instructions for making stuffed figures on page 5.

Fold the fabric for the gingerbread man in half and trace the pattern.

If you want to make gingerbread men to decorate a picture, hang on the Christmas tree or as a wreath, trace the pattern with feet and sew around the whole figure, see figure A. Cut an opening for turning the fabric through, in one of the fabric layers.

If the gingerbread men are intended to be placed in a cookie jar or tin, follow the dotted line instead of the legs, and make an opening in the seam, see figure B.

Cut out, turn the right way out, iron, fill with stuffing and stitch the openings as described on page 5 and 6.

Sew a couple of crosses on the gingerbread man with three strands of embroidery yarn or a double sewing thread, or stitch on three red beads for buttons. Another option is appliquéing a heart on the gingerbread figure, see appliqués on page 34.

Perfect bows

Cut along the grain of the fabric to make long strips about 1.7 x 18cm (1 x 7in) long, and cut another piece of the same width, but only 2.5cm (1in) long. Fold the long strip as shown in figure C, – the finished bow should be about 6cm (2½in) across. Tie up the bow with sewing cotton, see figure D. Fold the short strip of fabric in half lengthways and fix around the bow with a little glue, see figure E. Glue or stitch the bow on to the figure, and make a face as described on page 6.

A

B

C 6 cm

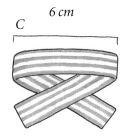

D

E

The kitchen should be decorated in honour of the person who cooks all the good food, perhaps using gingerbread men as a motif. These little 'cookies' will keep for years, and they never date.

Gingerbread men decoration

Pattern given on page 92.

You will need:

- a biscuit tin or similar, at least 10cm (4in) tall
- gingerbread men without feet, see instructions on page 58
- medium-sized padded heart, see page 27
- plant stick or similar
- tea towel or fabric to decorate the edge of the tin
- little stars, beads and thin steel wire for decorating
- embroidery threads and fabric paints for the face

This is how you do it:

Cut a strip of tea towel or fabric about 10cm (4in) wide, and glue the wrong side to the inside of the tin. Fold the rest of the strip over the top edge of the tin, so that the right side of the tea towel, with the hemmed edge, hangs down on the outside. See the picture below.

Make a medium-sized padded heart, see page 27, and fix it on a stick. Make three or four gingerbread men with bows or appliqué hearts and insert as many as the opening in the tin will take, and push the heart on a stick down at the back. Tuck a little stuffing in between the figures to make sure they sit well.

Attach little stars or beads to a length of thin steel wire and weave it around the decoration.

For the frost effect, see page 7.

Instead of a biscuit tin you can use a box, basket or flower pot to fill with little gingerbread men.

A wreath is made by stitching the arms of five gingerbread men together in a row. Attach a plastic ring at either end to hang it from. If you wish, you can fasten thin twigs at the back of the wreath, and glue on red berries and white stars to decorate them.

The frost effect is described on page 7.

Little snowmen and snow angels

Pattern given on page 93.

You will need:

- natural white cotton for the body and arms
- stuffing
- plastic granules (optional)
- fabrics for the scarves
- buttons for ear-muffs or twigs, thin wire and red beads for the wreath
- fabric and wadding for the wings
- embroidery threads and fabric paints for the face
- Christmas trees, see page 69

This is how you do it:

Read the general instructions for making stuffed figures on page 5.

Fold the fabric for the arms and body in half, right sides together, and trace the pattern. Sew around them, see figure A. Cut out the pieces. To make a base for the snowman which will allow him to stand upright, match the side and bottom seams and stitch across so that points A and B on the pattern meet, see figure B. Cut away the corners outside the seam.

Make an opening in one of the fabric layers of each arm for turning the fabric inside out, as shown on the pattern. Make sure the openings are on different sides so you have a left and right arm, see figure C.

Turn right sides out, iron, fill with stuffing and close the openings.

If you want the snowman to stand upright on its own, add some plastic granules at the bottom of the body after stuffing. Tack the opening closed.

Make a scarf as described on page 15, and tie it on the snowman before stitching on the arms. Make a face for the figure as described on page 6, and sew crosses down the front using black sewing cotton, see figure D.

If you wish, you can sew on two buttons for ear-muffs, add a padded heart under one arm or make small wings as described on page 17 and make a wreath as described on page 18. Glue or stitch the wings, heart and wreath on to the snowman.

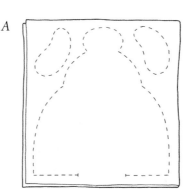

A

B

C

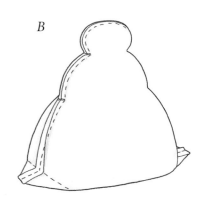

D

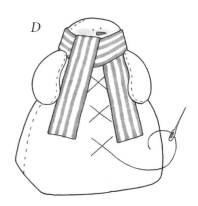

Flower pot snowmen

Create a focal point in a window by placing snowmen or snow angels in painted terracotta pots.

The big pot with the snow angels measures 18cm (7in) across and the small pot featuring one snowman is 13cm (5in) across. The pots have been brushed with brown paint and the tops sponged with white paint to create a snowy effect.

Fill the pots with blocks of oasis before gluing the figure(s) on top. Make a little Christmas tree as described on page 69, and push this into the oasis behind the figures. Glue some stuffing around the top to look like snow, and add the frost effect as described on page 7. For how to make the little hearts, see page 27.

E

Snow angel garland

The snow angels for the garland have their arms stitched to the back of their bodies so that they stick out on both sides. The opening for turning the fabric inside out should be on the back of the figure and is hidden by the wings. Stitch the wings on to both the body and the arms, to make sure the parts hang together, see figure E.

By stitching together three snow angels, with medium-sized hearts in between, see page 27, you will get a slightly longer garland. Attach a plastic ring on each side to hang it from, and some thin twigs at the back of the angels to decorate. For adding a frost effect, see page 7.

65

Penguins are known to stay together in families, so it might be nice to make a group of figures, taking one's own family as the starting point. We have patterns for three sizes, so all your family members can be included.

Penguins

Patterns given on pages 92, 94 and 95.

You will need:
- black and natural cotton fabric for the body
- plastic granules (optional)
- double-sided interfacing
- stuffing
- fabric for the scarf or bow
- buttons for the ear-muffs
- embroidery threads and fabric paints for the face

A

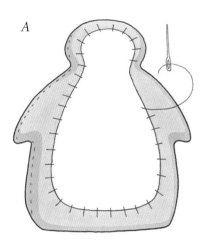

This is how you do it:

Read the general instruction for making stuffed figures on page 5.

Fold the black fabric for the body in half, trace the pattern in the size you want, and sew around it.

Cut out the figure and make a base by following the instructions for the snowman on page 62.

Turn the right way out and press.

Iron interfacing on to the wrong side of the white fabric and remove the paper. Trace and cut out the front piece. Iron the front on to the figure and whipstitch around it, using double, white sewing thread, see figure A.

Fill with stuffing, using some plastic granules at the bottom if you would like the figure to stand up on its own and sew the opening closed.

Make the scarf as described on page 15, and add the face and beak as described on page 6.

The bow for the gingerbread men on page 58 will fit the little penguin.

Penguin wreath

A medium-sized penguin and two little ones have been glued to a wreath measuring about 35cm (14in) across. It makes a humorous and slightly different decoration for a door. Use an ice lolly stick or similar, to support the medium-sized penguin and help it stand upright.

The wreath and the penguins have been dusted with frost, following the technique described on page 7. A little raffia bow and a ribbon with some red berries, are added as a decoration.

Christmas decorations with little penguins sitting in terracotta plant pots are made the same way as the decorations with the snowmen and snow angels on page 62. The pot with the two penguins measures 15cm (6in) across and the pot with an angel penguin is 11cm (4½in) across.

Christmas trees

Patterns given on pages 91 and 93.

You will need:
- light green linen or similar fabric for trees
- stuffing
- 3-4mm($\frac{1}{8}$in) diameter plant stick
- small hearts, see page 27
- flowerpot, oasis and fine wood wool

A

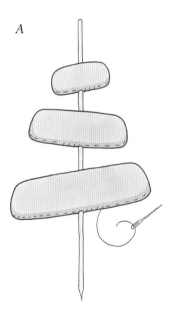

This is how you do it

Read the general instructions for making stuffed figures on page 5.

The large Christmas trees, decorated with hearts, make attractive decorations in their own right. The small Christmas trees look good in combination with figures such as the snowmen and penguins.

Fold a piece of fabric in half and trace the pattern for either a large or a small Christmas tree. Mark the openings and sew around the pieces.

Cut out, iron, turn out and fill with stuffing. Push a sharpened plant stick through the openings in the Christmas tree pieces. Twist the stick while pushing it through, to avoid taking too much stuffing material with it.

Tack the openings around the plant stick firmly closed, so that the three pieces lean in different directions, see figure A.

Attach little padded hearts or beads to decorate, according to your preference. Run a line of stitching around each piece using three strands of embroidery thread. Push the tree into a pot filled with oasis and cover the oasis with fine wood wool, or something similar.

Painted Christmas motifs

The appliqué motifs can also be used for painted decorations, and the smaller motifs are ideal for use on cards.

This is how you do it:

Start off by mixing the background colour you want. The boxes have been painted with a mixture of white and midnight blue. Only a touch of blue is needed to make this very pale blue shade. The background area on the tray has been painted with a mixture of white and teddy brown. Here too, just a little colour is added to the white, to keep the shade light.

Make sure you mix enough colour for the background, and keep any left over so that you can touch up any mistakes you might make when painting the design.

Trace the motifs on to the background and fill the areas with colour.

Some of the presents have been painted using the light blue background colour that has been used for the boxes, and others along with the ear-muffs have been painted in a slightly darker version of the tray's background colour. The ear-muffs for the snowman on the box have been painted using a mix of lilac and white.

To achieve some variation in the red colours, some areas have been painted with red mixed with white, while the rest have been filled in with just red.

The holly leaves have been painted using spring green and dark moss green and the birds are midnight blue and dark moss green.

Painting stripes

Draw up the stripes, using a ruler if you prefer, and begin by filling in the stripes with the lightest colour.

Then fill every other stripe with the darker colour.

Painting checks

The gingham checks consist of three colours, and it is often easiest to begin with the middle colour. Mix white with the dark colour to make an in-between shade, and use it to paint the whole area. Draw in the checks, using a ruler if you like, and fill in the white squares, see figure A. Then fill in the dark squares, see figure B.

Frost

The motifs have been given a frost effect at the end, to give the design a nice wintry feel.

Dip a dry brush into some white paint, and dab it off on a piece of paper so that only a little of the colour remains on the brush. Brush the paint lightly on to the figures in the design by moving the brush swiftly to and fro.

Details

Paint the noses and beaks using terra-cotta and draw the eyes, crosses and decorative stitching with the black pen. The roses for the cheeks can be made as described on page 7.

When all the paints are completely dry, varnish the picture, box or tray.

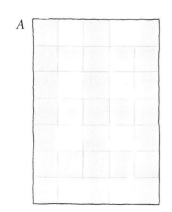

A

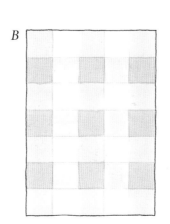

B

Craft ball snowmen

This is how you do it

Table decoration

Glue the snowmen and snowballs on to a wood base, and paint the whole of the decoration with white paint.

Make scarves as described on page 15, and tie them round the necks of the snowmen.

Cut the knitted socks for the hats, turn inside out and stitch one end, before turning right way out again. Fold in the edge around the opening of the hat, and glue it to the figure.

Make faces as described on page 6, and glue buttons on for ear-muffs. Make holes in the snowman's sides using an awl or a small screwdriver and glue the arms into the holes.

Cut the ends of the lolly sticks into points to form a picket fence and paint them with a mixture of midnight blue and white.

Glue the fence to the edge of the base. Use glue to fasten the wood wool, spade and stars, and add a frost effect as described on page 7.

Snowman boxes

The head of the snowman should be in proportion to the size of the box. Glue the craft ball for the head to the lid, and paint the head and box white. Glue on the twig arms and paint crosses down the front of the box. Tie on the scarves, add hats, paint the faces and add a frost effect as for the table decoration.

A bigger box could have a single snowman with snowballs. The one in the picture above has a strip of fabric round the base.

Paper cornets

Pattern given on page 84.

You will need:

- sheet of decorated card larger than A4 in size
- tissue paper
- glue
- adhesive tape and a hole punch
- narrow ribbons

This is how you do it:

Use the template for the cornet angels. The pattern should be traced twice with the folded edge in the middle. Add a thin edge for gluing on one side, see figure A below.

Put some glue on the glue edge and shape into a cornet. A little adhesive tape may be needed on the inside to hold the cornet together. Make a hole on either side of the cornet and tie on a ribbon for hanging. Arrange a little tissue paper inside the cornet, and fill it up with Christmas sweets.

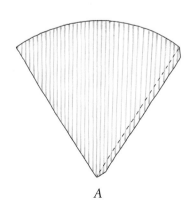

A

Christmas cards and gift tags

Pattern given on page 91

You will need:

- Card, coloured on one side, or ready-made card blanks
- various bits of decorated paper and card for the motifs
- a small, pointed pair of scissors
- small buttons
- raffia
- tiny red beads for holly berries
- crystal-coloured glitter pen
- fine black pen
- hole punch
- double-sided sticky pads
- PVA glue and a stronger glue for the beads
- white paint and a large-headed pin for the snowflakes
- fabric and interfacing
- small padded heart

This is how you do it:

The gift tags measure 13 x 7cm (5 x 3in) and the cards are 24 x 17cm (9½ x 7in) before being folded.

Trace the pattern pieces for the motif on to card or paper and cut out.

Cards

Glue the background panel and two of the parcels directly on to the card.

Glue scarf, button ear-muffs, carrot nose or beak and a parcel on to the figure. Draw in the eyes and crosses with a black pen and add stitches round the panel. Paint the rosy cheeks as described on page 6.

Glue the sticky pads to the back of the figure, and stick it on to the card so that it stands out. Glue on some red beads for berries on the holly leaves, and decorate the motif with the glitter pen.

Dip the pin head in white paint and print snowflakes over the background.

Gift tags

Make a hole for the raffia strings using a hole punch. Glue the holly leaves directly on to the card, and fix the parcel using sticky pads. Glue on red beads for berries, and use a glitter pen to decorate.

Heart cards

Iron interfacing on to the wrong side of a piece of fabric to stop the raw edges from fraying, and remove the paper. Cut out piece measuring about 7.5 x 6cm (3 x 3½in), and sew it on to the card using the zig-zag stitch on the sewing machine. Finally, glue on a small padded heart, see page 27.

It is much nicer, and often more economical, to make your own Christmas cards and gift tags, rather than buying them. Besides, most recipients are really pleased to get something homemade.

Patterns

All patterns one full size, but seam allowance must be added to all the pattern pieces, except when making appliqués, cards and noses for the figures.

ROCKING REINDEER

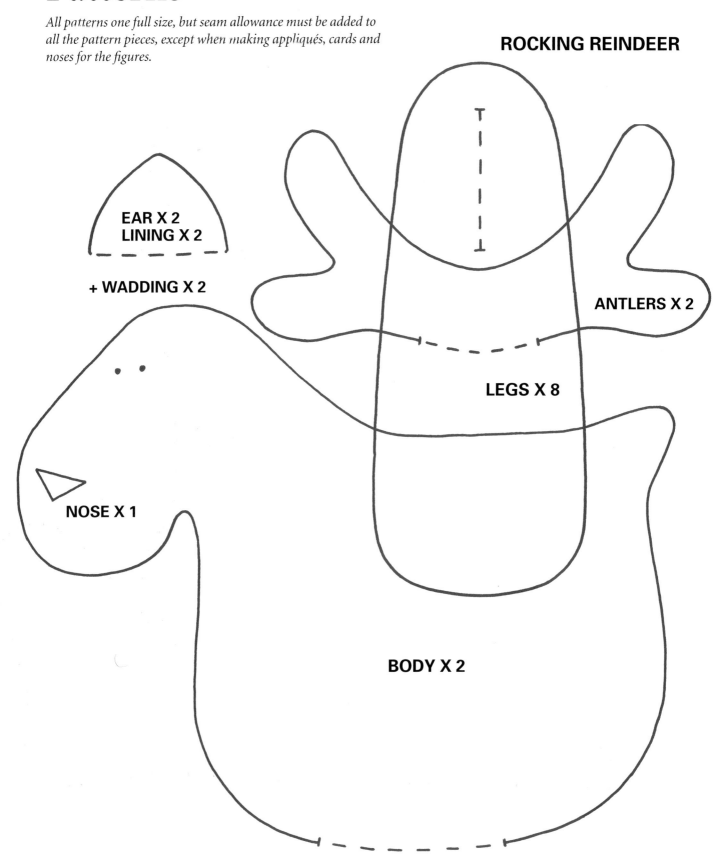

EAR X 2
LINING X 2

+ WADDING X 2

ANTLERS X 2

LEGS X 8

NOSE X 1

BODY X 2

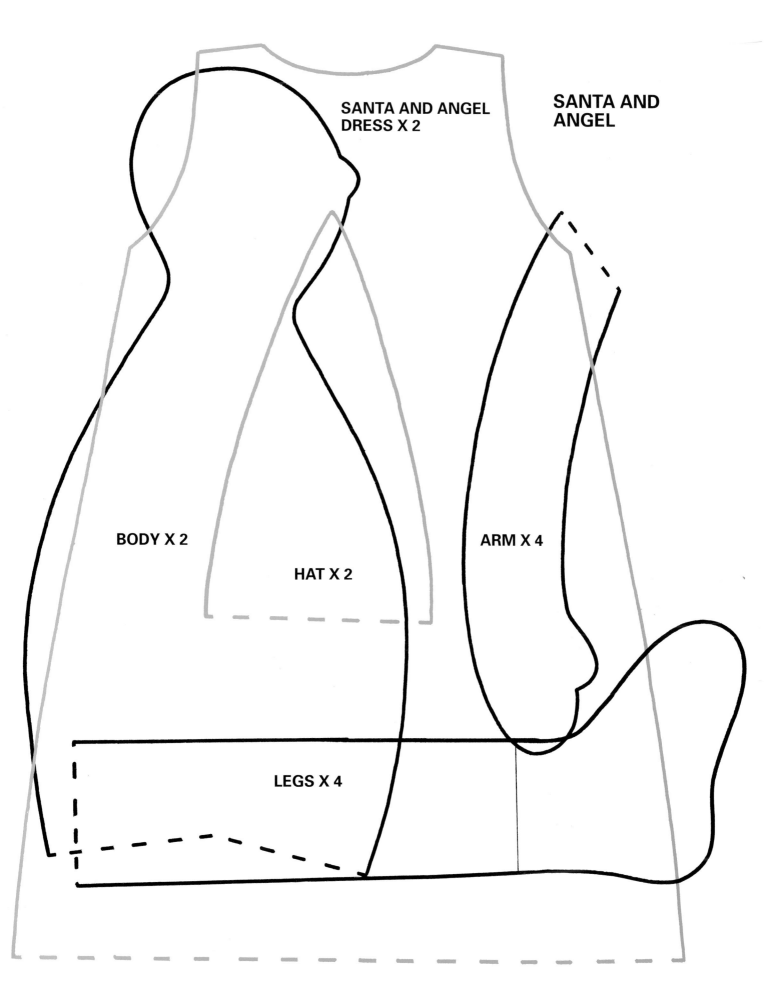

SANTA AND ANGEL
DRESS X 2

SANTA AND
ANGEL

BODY X 2

HAT X 2

ARM X 4

LEGS X 4

77

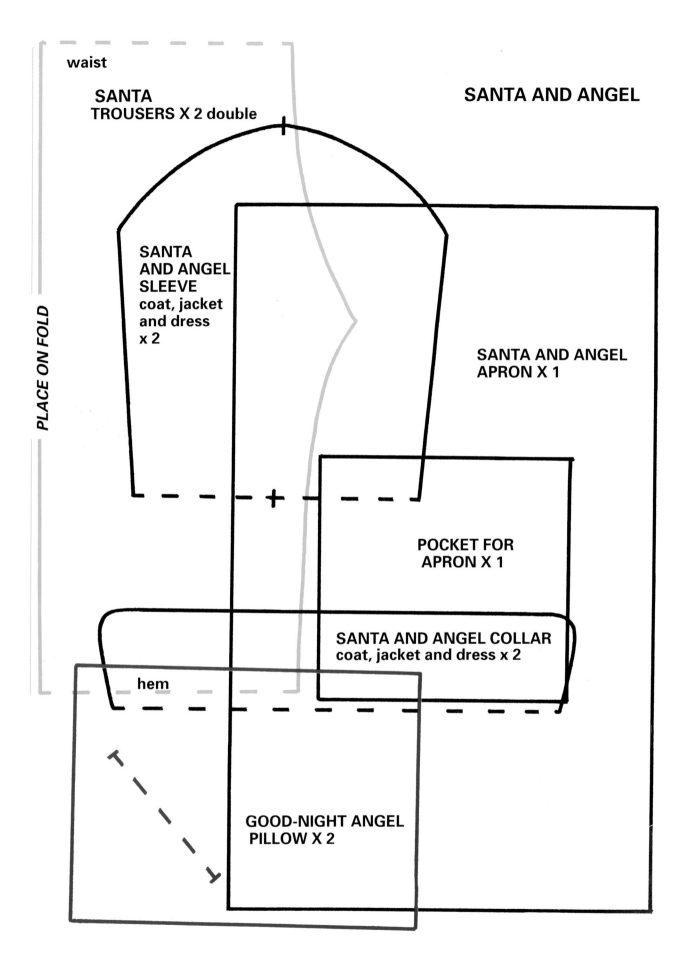

waist

SANTA
TROUSERS X 2 double

SANTA AND ANGEL

PLACE ON FOLD

**SANTA
AND ANGEL
SLEEVE
coat, jacket
and dress
x 2**

**SANTA AND ANGEL
APRON X 1**

**POCKET FOR
APRON X 1**

**SANTA AND ANGEL COLLAR
coat, jacket and dress x 2**

hem

**GOOD-NIGHT ANGEL
PILLOW X 2**

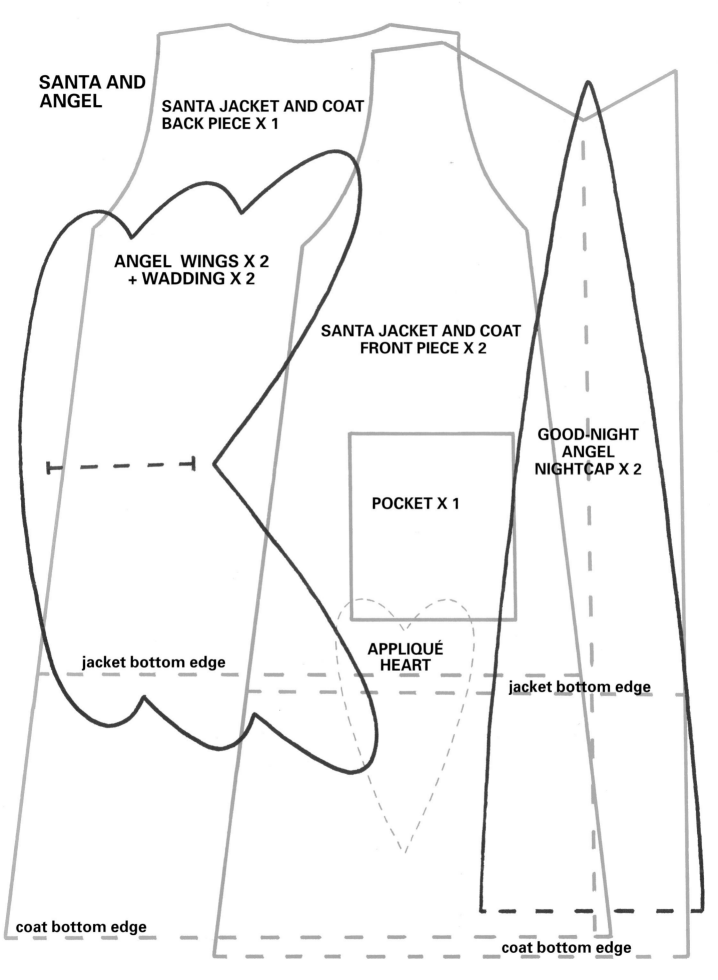

SANTA AND ANGEL

SANTA JACKET AND COAT
BACK PIECE X 1

ANGEL WINGS X 2
+ WADDING X 2

SANTA JACKET AND COAT
FRONT PIECE X 2

GOOD-NIGHT
ANGEL
NIGHTCAP X 2

POCKET X 1

jacket bottom edge

APPLIQUÉ
HEART

jacket bottom edge

coat bottom edge

coat bottom edge

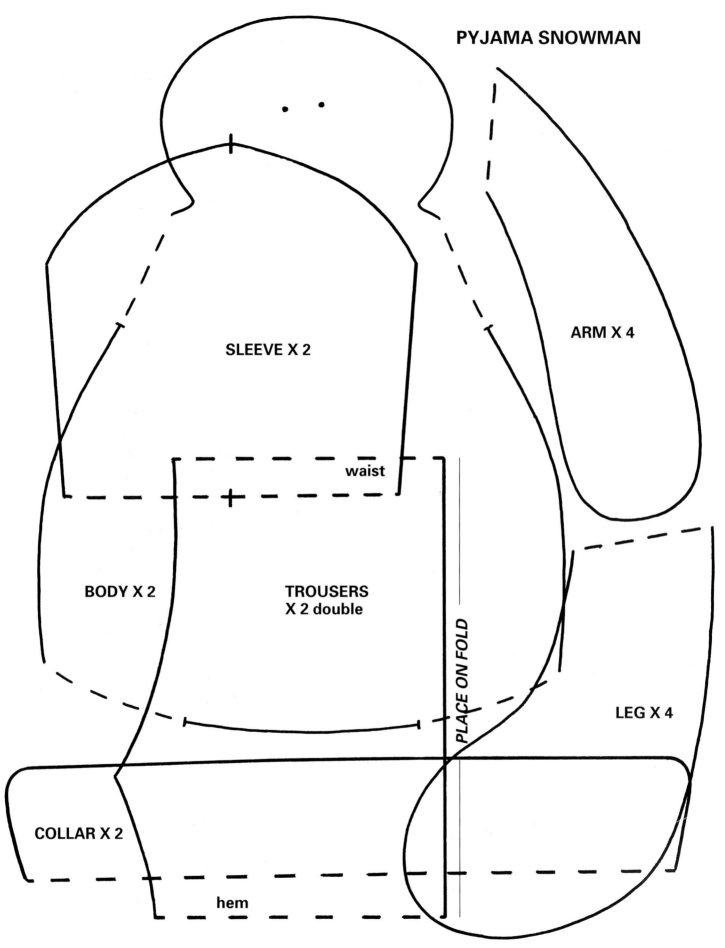

PYJAMA SNOWMAN

SLEEVE X 2

ARM X 4

waist

BODY X 2

TROUSERS
X 2 double

PLACE ON FOLD

LEG X 4

COLLAR X 2

hem

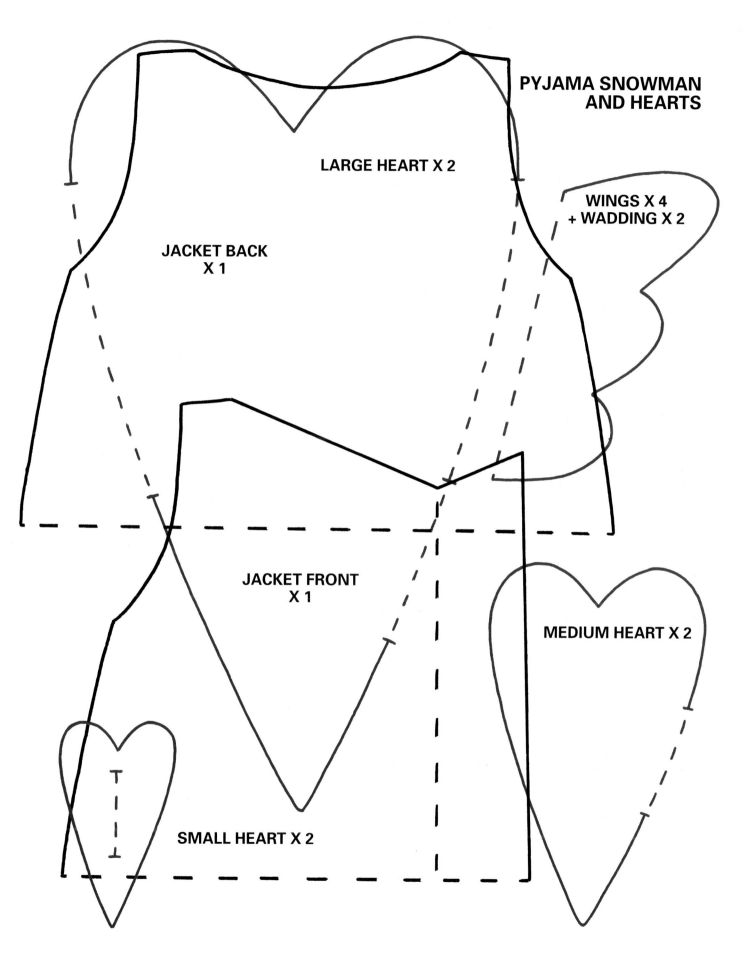

PYJAMA SNOWMAN AND HEARTS

LARGE HEART X 2

WINGS X 4
+ WADDING X 2

JACKET BACK
X 1

JACKET FRONT
X 1

MEDIUM HEART X 2

SMALL HEART X 2

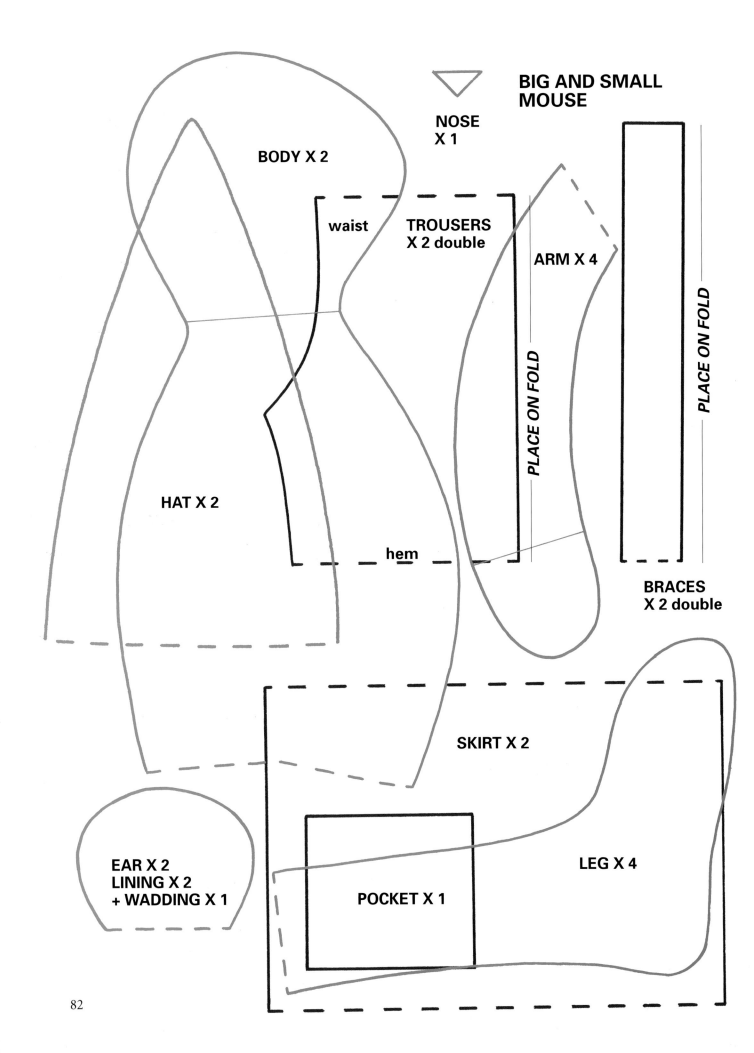

BIG AND SMALL MOUSE

NOSE X 1

BODY X 2

waist

TROUSERS X 2 double

ARM X 4

PLACE ON FOLD

PLACE ON FOLD

HAT X 2

hem

BRACES X 2 double

SKIRT X 2

EAR X 2
LINING X 2
+ WADDING X 1

POCKET X 1

LEG X 4

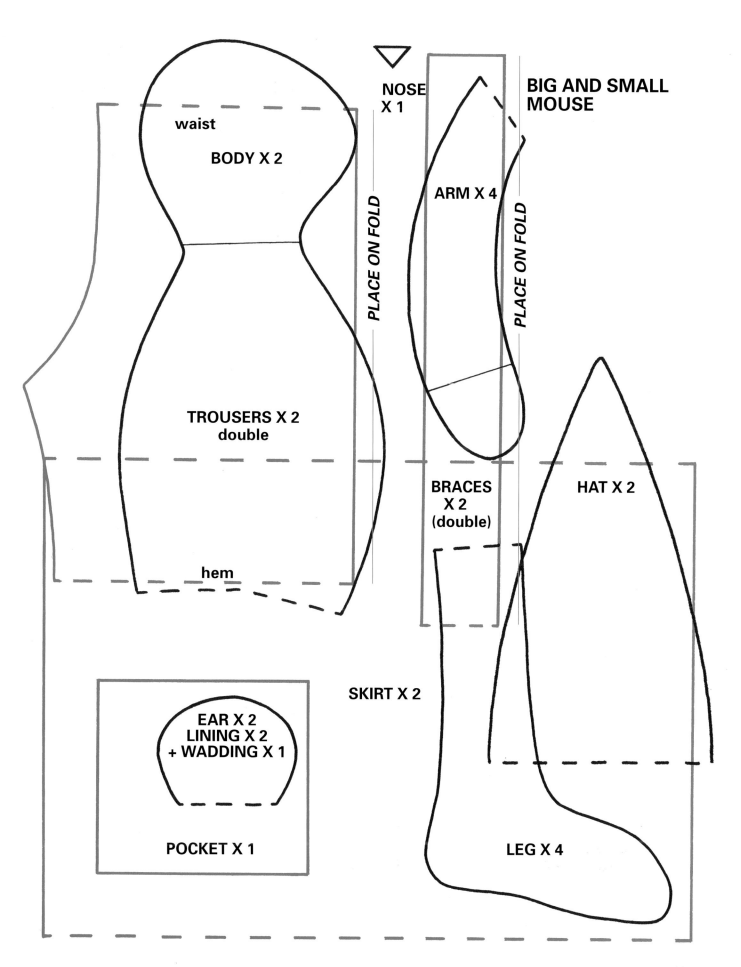

NOSE X 1

BIG AND SMALL MOUSE

waist

BODY X 2

ARM X 4

PLACE ON FOLD

PLACE ON FOLD

TROUSERS X 2
double

BRACES
X 2
(double)

HAT X 2

hem

SKIRT X 2

EAR X 2
LINING X 2
+ WADDING X 1

POCKET X 1

LEG X 4

83

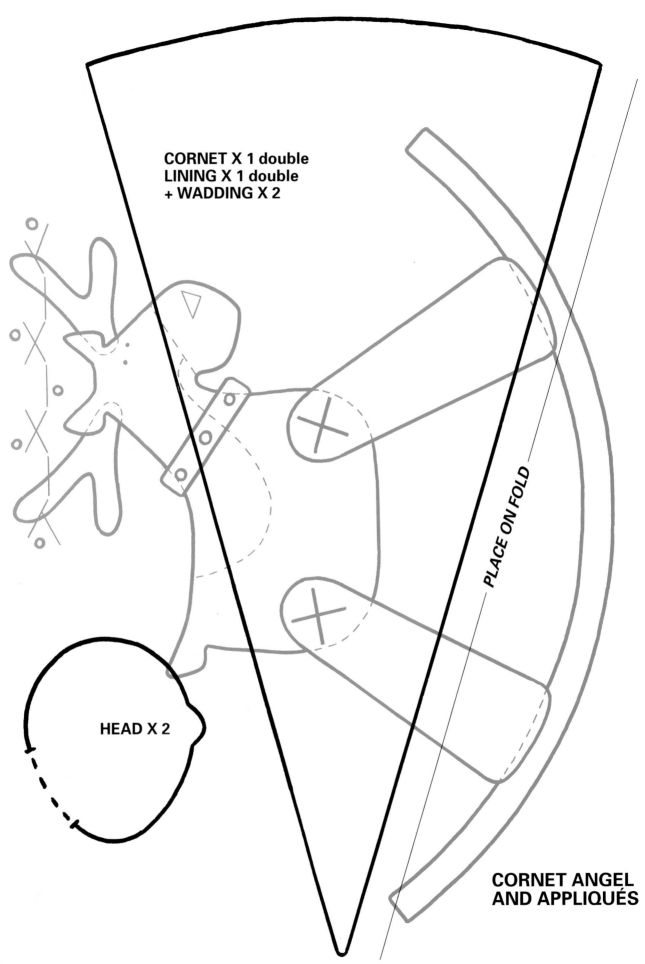

CORNET X 1 double
LINING X 1 double
+ WADDING X 2

HEAD X 2

PLACE ON FOLD

CORNET ANGEL
AND APPLIQUÉS

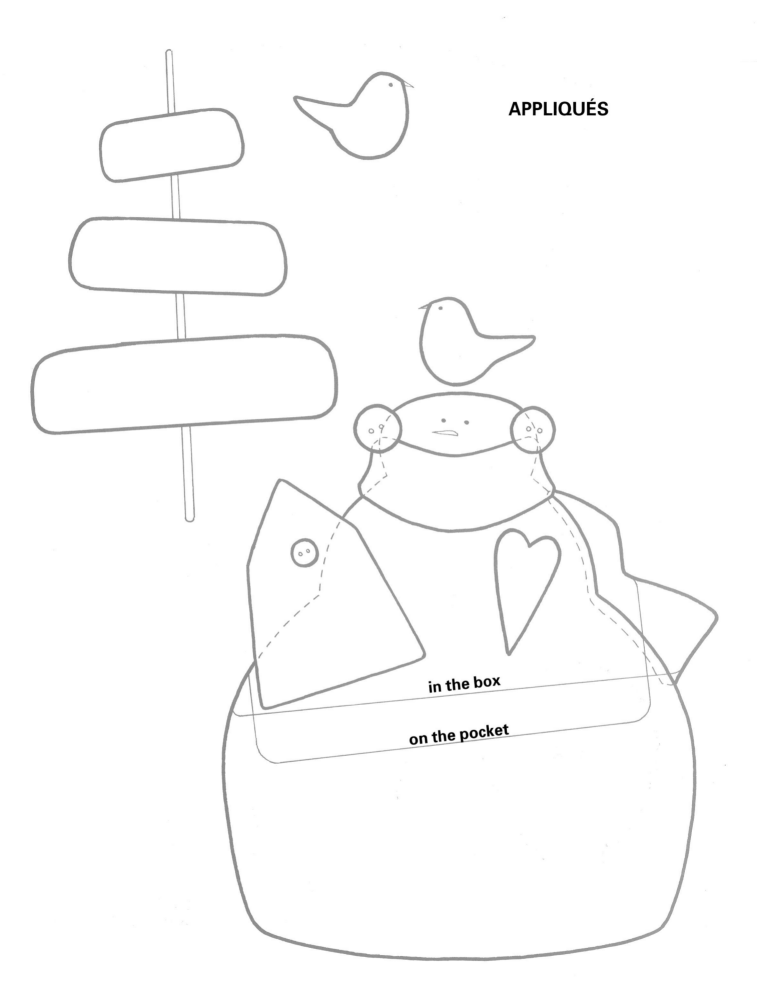

in the box

on the pocket

APPLIQUÉS

GOD JUL

(GOD JUL
= MERRY
CHRISTMAS)

in the box

on the pocket

APPLIQUÉS

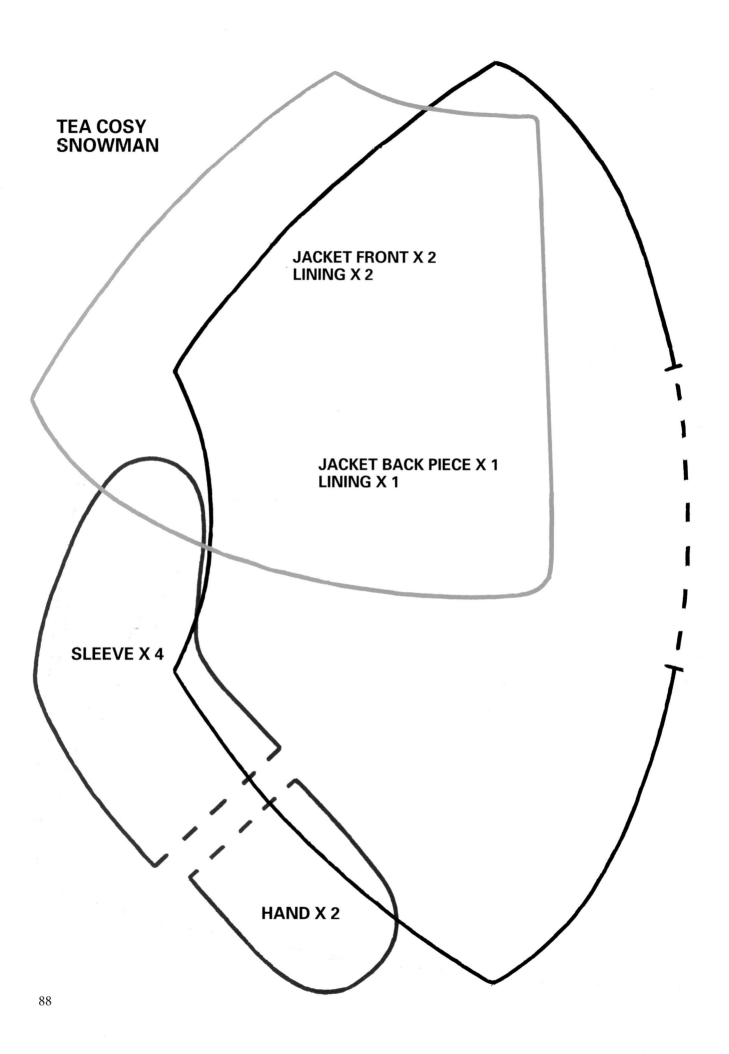

**TEA COSY
SNOWMAN**

**JACKET FRONT X 2
LINING X 2**

**JACKET BACK PIECE X 1
LINING X 1**

SLEEVE X 4

HAND X 2

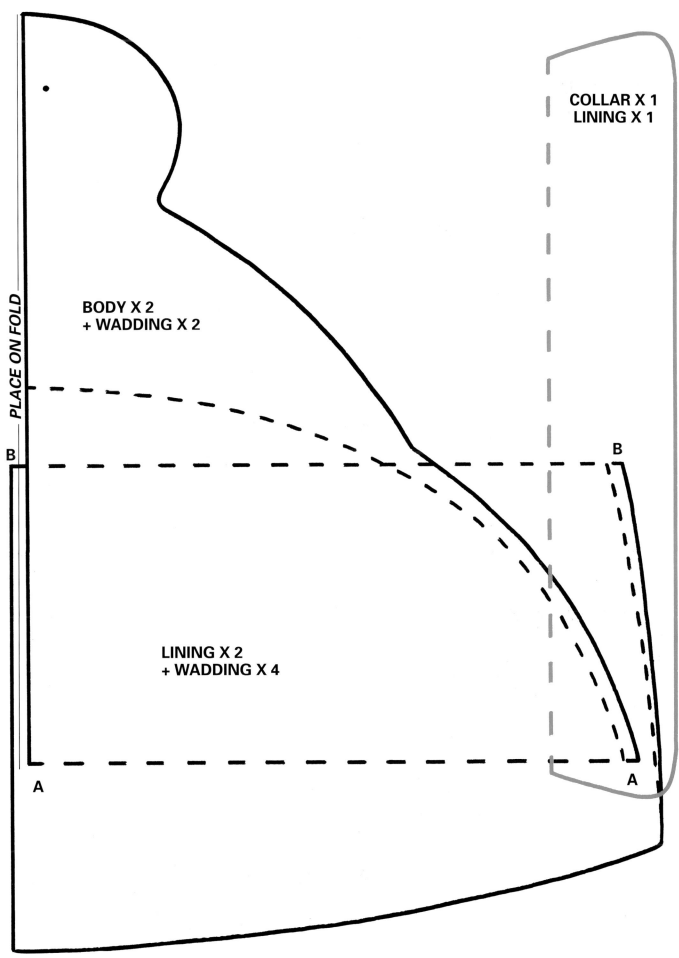

PLACE ON FOLD

BODY X 2
+ WADDING X 2

LINING X 2
+ WADDING X 4

COLLAR X 1
LINING X 1

B

A

B

A

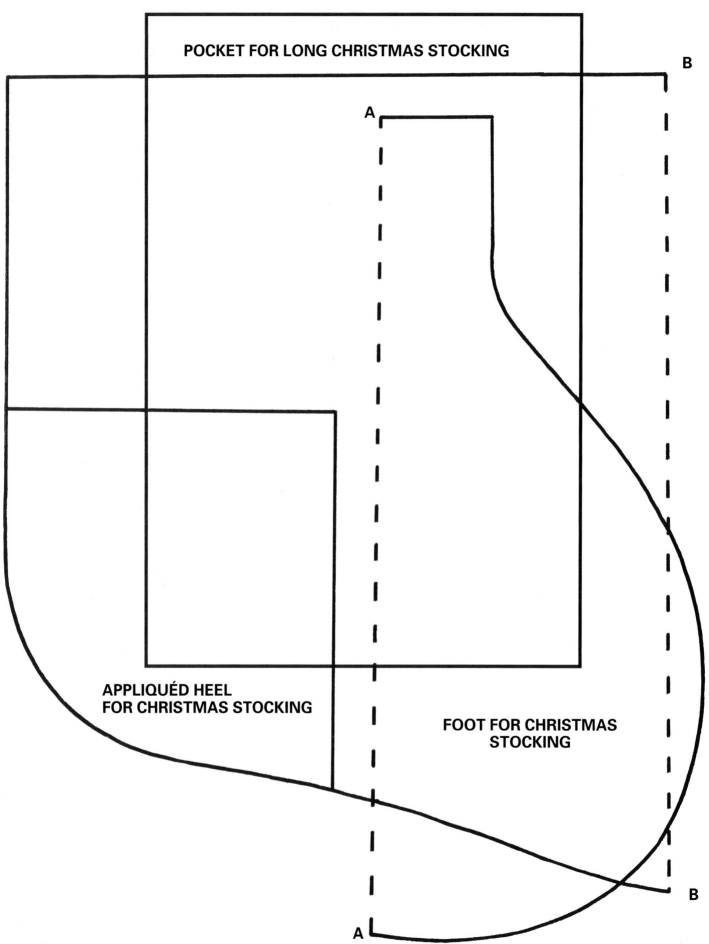

POCKET FOR LONG CHRISTMAS STOCKING

B

A

APPLIQUÉD HEEL
FOR CHRISTMAS STOCKING

FOOT FOR CHRISTMAS
STOCKING

B

A

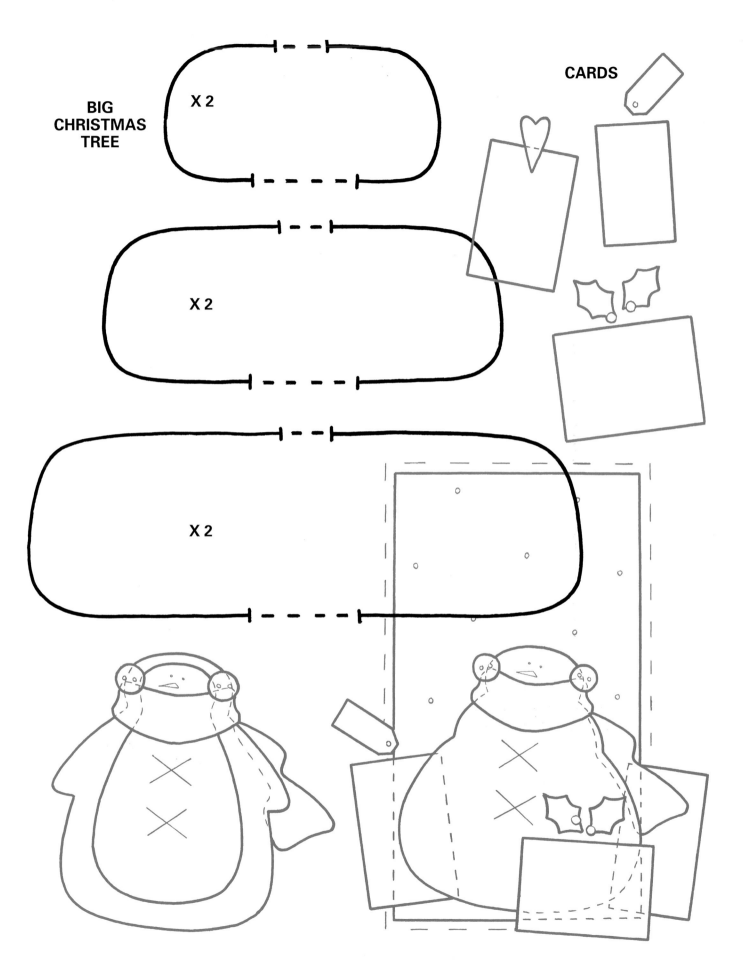

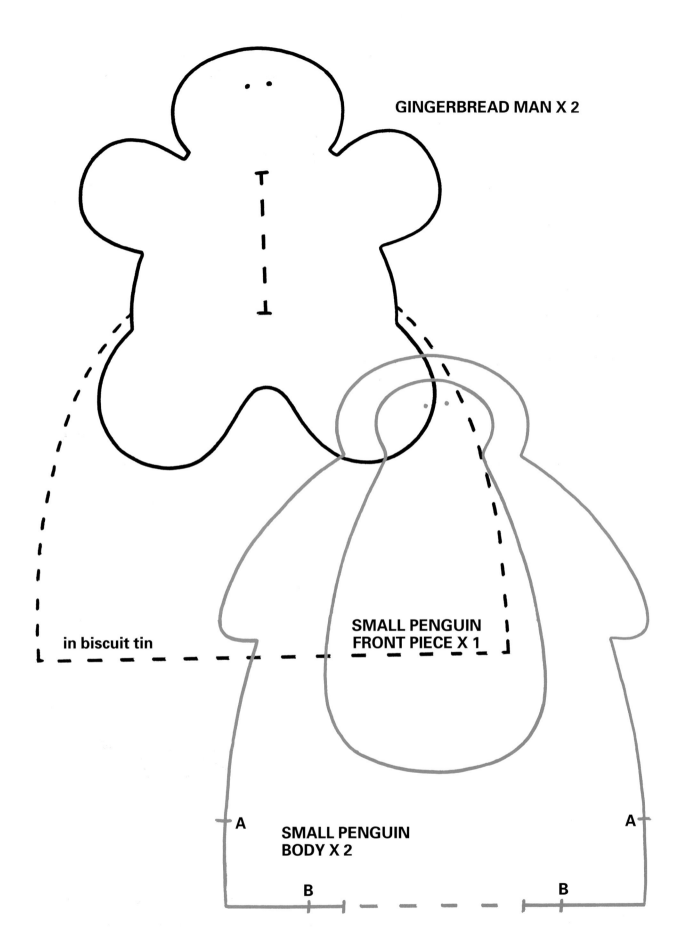

GINGERBREAD MAN X 2

in biscuit tin

**SMALL PENGUIN
FRONT PIECE X 1**

A   A

**SMALL PENGUIN
BODY X 2**

B   B

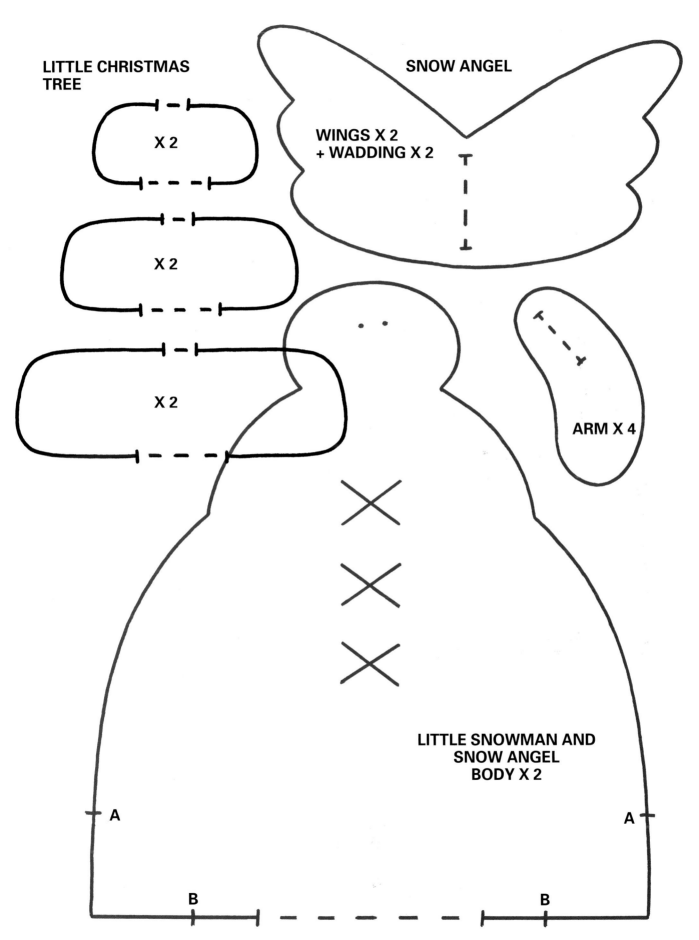

LITTLE CHRISTMAS TREE

X 2

X 2

X 2

SNOW ANGEL

**WINGS X 2
+ WADDING X 2**

ARM X 4

**LITTLE SNOWMAN AND
SNOW ANGEL
BODY X 2**

A

A

B

B

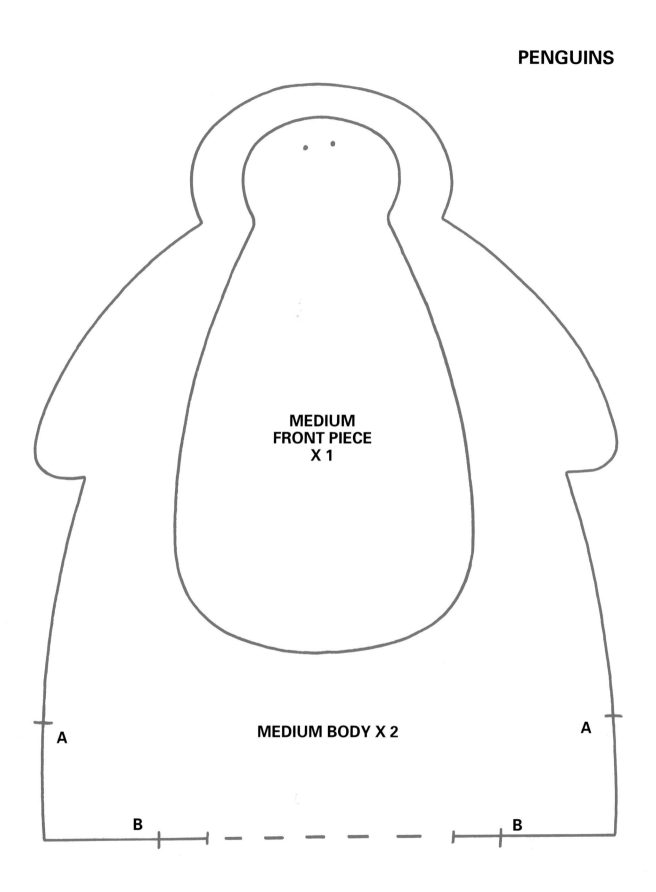

MEDIUM
FRONT PIECE
X 1

MEDIUM BODY X 2

A

A

B

B

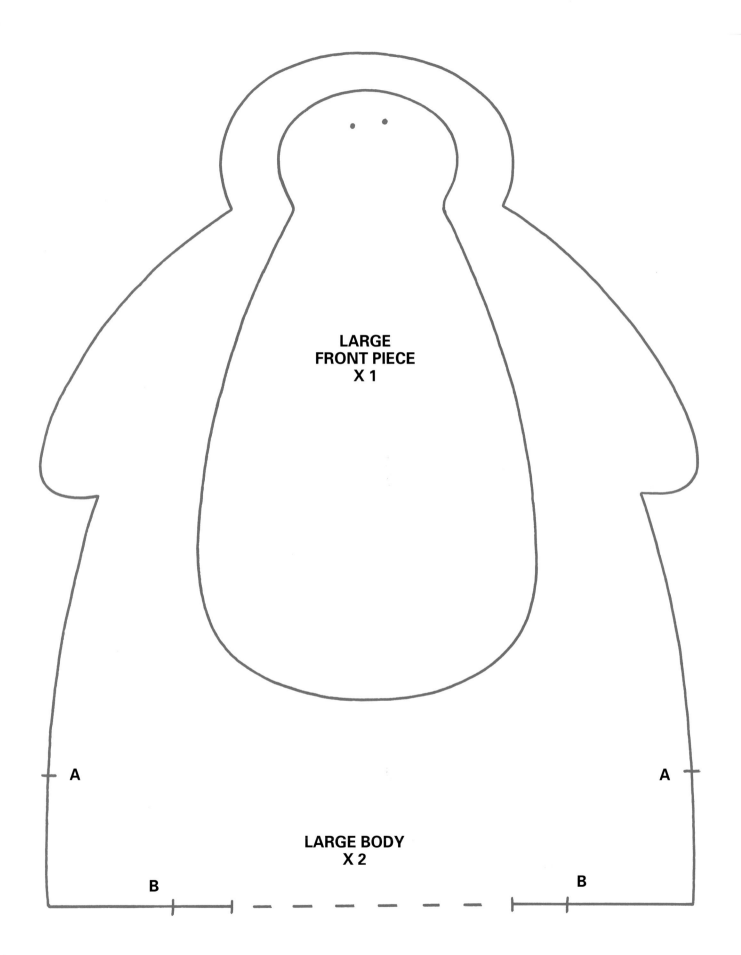

LARGE
FRONT PIECE
X 1

A

A

LARGE BODY
X 2

B

B

Suppliers

UK
Quilting materials
- The Bramble Patch
  West Street
  Weedon
  Northants NN7 4QU
  Tel: 01327 342212

- The Cotton Patch
  1285 Stratford Road
  Hall Green
  Birmingham B28 9AJ
  Tel: 0121 702 2840
  www.cottonpatch.net

Threads
- Coats Crafts UK
  PO Box 22
  Lingfield House
  McMullen Road
  Darlington
  Co Durham DL1 1YQ
  Tel: 01325 394237
  www.coatscrafts.co.uk

- DMC Creative World
  Pullman Road
  Wigston
  Leicester L18 2DY
  Tel: 0116 281 1040
  www.dmc/cw.com

Beads and sequins
- Ells & Farrier
  20 Beak Street
  London NW2 7JP
  Tel: 0207 629 9964

Fabrics
- Ragbags
  3 Kirkby Road
  Ripon
  N Yorkshire HG6 2EY
  www.ragbags.net

- Willow Fabrics
  95 Town Lane
  Mobberley
  Cheshire WA16 7HH
  Tel:0800 056 7811
  www.willowfabrics.com

- Fabric Flair Ltd
  The Old Brewery
  The Close
  Warminster, BA12 9AL
  Tel: 0800 716851

General embroidery supplies
- Voirrey Embroidery Centre
  Brimstage Hall
  Wirral L63 6JA
  Tel: 0151 342 3514

USA
Threads
- Coats and Clark USA
  PO Box 12229
  Greenville
  SC29612-0229
  Tel: (800) 648 1479
  www.coatsandclark.com